STRIDE

SELF-CARE *for*

BLACK WOMEN

OVER

50

NIA J. RIVERS

All in all, you are just hitting your stride, and hopefully, through these upcoming chapters, you can stand ten toes down as the world's crown jewel that we all are.

– Nia J. Rivers, 2023

part of a legacy of great and powerful women and each of us carries the mantle handed to us by our ancestors. Black women are the Alpha of humanity, with a wealth of experience and stories that can carry us all through to the next century. This is a legacy that our mothers handed over to us before they left this world.

And so here you are, reading this introduction and wondering, *what's next?*

Within these pages, you will find reminders of your own divine femininity. You will learn that aging isn't something that should be avoided, but rather, it should be embraced. You will receive advice on cultivating the garden of your own wisdom, personality, and grace and being comfortable with who you are and who you were always meant to be. Tips on your physical and mental health, your community life, and your legacy will help you to understand that life after fifty doesn't mean the end of the road.

By the end of this book, you'll get to understand the contributions you make to the next generation through cultivating your legacy, examining and sharing the stories of our ancestors, and through our contributions to the society in which we live.

of us, aging means changes in our bodies, minds, and our places within our communities. And if you've ever been to your place of worship and had someone of the younger generation call you 'ma'am' or some other aged-based honorific, then you understand how jarring it is to realize that you are now considered "old" by your peers.

If you're like me, you probably have started evaluating the next chapter of your life and what that will look like. For me, the first thing that came to my mind was that, above all, I wanted to be happy and fulfilled. I mean, yeah, I'd like to stop the aging process in every way possible. Who doesn't? But that's not realistic. Time marches on, ladies, and like it or not, we've got to march with it.

I started searching and researching what was out there and what that meant for women like me, and what I found is that a lot of you are in the same boat as I am. We are black women who are finding ourselves in a different world than the one we started in, and it seems like the rules have changed for us. With everything that we are and everything that we must endure, we must all find a new place to be who we really are *and* be happy in it.

What I came to realize is that, yes, the rules have changed, but not in the ways we might think. We are a my own individuality, I never thought of myself as having to adhere to the whims of the common philosophy on a black woman's place in the world. I've always done my own thing with my mother's encouragement.

But my journey through aging has been different than hers. I started to focus on the negative aspects of aging. Physically, I had to deal with achy joints and muscles. Suddenly, my blood pressure was up and my calcium was down. I also started to see my position in life change. My children were all adults and getting on with their lives. My role of mother shifted to grandmother, and suddenly, I was given a whole new set of rules of life to live by.

And as all these things started to happen to me, I began to wonder if this chapter of my life would be the same as my mother's. Now, I was getting *old* too. It felt like it came out of nowhere. I certainly never *felt* old, yet here I was. It was like coming home to find "old" sitting on your couch with its feet on the coffee table and eating your food. You want to yell at it and ask, *How did you get in here??*

Being "old" represents a lot of things to a lot of people. In fact, I know a lot of women who refuse to even call themselves old in the first place, preferring alternate words like "mature" as if the word itself were a curse. For most unless it was a political statement), and she lived in blue jeans and belt buckles. She danced to musical artists like Parliament and Aerosmith with equal steps. And much to the dismay of my grandmother, my mom loved to dance and drink at parties, and she was known to tell a good dirty joke from time to time.

Suffice it to say that my mom always loved life and everything about it. She is, and always has been, the life of the party at gatherings. She laughs loudly, speaks freely, and explores the world on her own terms. Forever the nomad, my mom has traveled to every part of the United States and even a few countries abroad. She's never let anything slow her down.

Perhaps it was this exposure that made her so progressive in her thinking about herself and her place in a world that often disregarded and disparaged black women for falling out of line with the steps of the rest of the community. It seemed that when the elders of our family told her she couldn't do something, that was all she needed to hear to do it anyway. She never allowed anything to get in the way of being whoever she wanted to be, however she wanted to do it.

These days, I think about her a lot now that I'm getting up there in age. Even though she raised me to embrace

Introduction

"Life is for living, so live!"
— *Miriam Johnson*

The above quote is attributed to my mother, Ms. Miriam. The matriarchs of her generation often called her a "free spirit." This word was a polite way of describing a woman of my mother's unique temperament. My grandmother and great-grandmother would look at a woman like Ms. Miriam and had no other way of defining her so-called wild ways and "free-spirited" was the only way to describe her.

When my mom was young, she could see no reason to abide by the unspoken rules placed upon young black women of her day. As a teenager, my mother wore her hair in a huge "natural" (they didn't call them Afros back then

Contents

To the spirited Black women
Who have inspired and uplifted me throughout my life
This book is a tribute to your strength, grace, and unyielding spirit
I offer a heartfelt celebration of self-care, dedicated to you all
Embrace these words as a reminder that your well-being is paramount
Your journey is worthy of care and celebration

PART ONE

Temple
Maintenance

CHAPTER ONE

Welcome to Your New Body

"Self-esteem means knowing
you are the dream."
— Oprah Winfrey

Your Temple Sets the Trends

Your body is an amazing creation. Have you ever considered the fact that, as black women, we walk around in bodies that are descended from the actual cradle of civilization? The first human remains were found in Ethiopia. Nicknamed Lucy, the remains are dated to be around 3.2 million years old (and recent discoveries date the fossils to be even older than that) (Handwerk 2022). This fascinating fact highlights the way our bodies have been the blueprint from the very beginning.

You've often heard the phrase "the body is a temple," and it's the truth when it comes to us. If you think about it, your body is as divine as any creation. It is a vessel for our fiery spirits. A living structure that reflects who we are to the outside world. Simply put, these bodies we live in are the temples for our souls.

But you can see it, right? Every time a white woman gets a BBL (Brazilian Butt Lift) or gets fillers for her lips, she mimics the features we naturally have. It doesn't stop there, either. From the style of our clothes to the diverse ways we style our hair, we have always been trendsetters.

But there's a saying, "Youth is wasted on the young," which implies we have a better understanding of all that when we're in our twenties and maybe even our thirties. It's only when we start to age that we begin to lose sight of the physical. And it's a trip when our spirit is still in its youth, but we start to experience all the physical and mental changes that come with getting older. So what does it all mean when we, as black women, start to age? If our temples are the trendsetters, how do we handle it when we start finding flaws and cracks in our beloved structure?

Your Temple's Curb Appeal

When I was sixteen, I had "En Vogue" legs, and I loved showing them off, especially in the summer. My legs were smooth and brown and thick in all the right ways, and let me tell you, in the summertime, I lived in short skirts and shorts. I fully understood the power of my own beautiful body and my self-esteem was way up as a result. I know and have known a lot of black women who have the same experience in their youths. In our culture, confidence was as valuable as currency. The girl with the thick legs who held her head up high was the girl who everyone wanted to hang out with.

But quiet as it's kept, that hasn't changed over the years. Here's another fun fact for you: In a recent survey conducted by *Glamour* magazine and L'Oréal Paris of over two thousand women across the nation, it appears that black women are already in their bag in terms of their self-esteem (Dreisbach 2017). Shaun Dreisbach's article states, "Black women consistently reported higher self-esteem than white or Hispanic women and—among other things—they were far more likely to describe themselves as successful." That statistic sounds pretty good, doesn't it? To put it succinctly, black women have the self-esteem game on lock.

Or do we? While that survey demonstrates a fundamental fact about black women in their view of themselves, where it's lacking is in the demographic...as in there doesn't seem to be one listed. In all the articles that cite this poll, there's an assumption that they aren't talking about us. And by us, I mean the us that picked up this book. My Gen Xers and Baby Boomers. Those of us who are reaching or have passed fifty years. They're not talking about us. They are talking about the self-esteem of young to middle-aged women, possibly between the ages of twenty-five and forty-five. So, what about women our age?

The old adage "Black don't crack" might be the culprit. We've been taught our entire lives that aging gracefully is just something that will just happen thanks to our high level of melanin. While that does slow the process down a little, it's not the end all be all. With age comes the wear and tear of weather and environment on our temples, so, like it or not, the sooner you start paying attention to the faults and cracks in your temple, the better you can manage them.

Your self-esteem is directly tied to your physical appearance. We want to look at ourselves in the morning and see the beautiful women that we truly are. Here are a few ways you can manage your temple's outward appearance:

- **Sunscreen. Every. Day.** While it doesn't do as much damage, it's a myth that the sun doesn't affect our skin at all. Personally, I recommend Black Girl Sunscreen, which protects without leaving white streaks on the skin (as with other sunscreens designed for lighter complexions).

- **Have hyperpigmentation and dark spots? Stay away from bleaching creams.** Outside of just being terrible for dark skin in every way imaginable, bleaching creams often do more to worsen hyperpigmentation and dark spots. And for anyone who's had a problem with either of those things, you most certainly don't want things to get any worse than they already are. In short, if you've got blotchy skin, do yourself a favor and leave it to the experts. Call a dermatologist for the source of why your skin is freaking out.

- **Drink water.** Seriously. Staying hydrated actually does wonders for the look of your skin. If you think you might not be getting enough water, pinch the back of your hand and observe how quickly the skin bounces back. If it sticks up too long, you need to increase your water intake. According to Mayo Clinic's guidelines for good health, adult women should drink 2.7 liters of water daily (Mayo Clinic 2022).

- **Lean into the changes instead of fighting them.** You can use creams and gels to stave off the wrinkles and pluck your gray hairs, but eventually, you're going to have to face up to the fact that you are aging. Now might be a good time to consider just dyeing your entire hair silver. (I hear it's all the rage these days).

Exercise Sucks...but Your Spirit Needs It

I will be the first to tell you how much I hate working out. I always have. I despise working out so much that I developed many negative thoughts surrounding it over the years. As in, I have to talk myself into getting on the treadmill every day. I have probably banked more time trying to talk myself out of working out than actually working out. I know that this isn't everyone's experience. Some people (like my son) relish the idea of a good workout every day. I am not one of those people.

Even though working out is the one thing I hate doing, I still do it every single day. And I could give you a laundry list of the physical benefits, but if I'm being honest, it's done wonders for my self-esteem in every way, especially now that I'm older. Physical health and self-esteem go hand in hand.

Any doctor will tell you that aging can increase the risk of developing chronic illnesses such as heart disease and diabetes and that exercise can help keep you free from those illnesses. Exercising can also be beneficial for your mental health as well. Maintaining a regular exercise regimen can promote better sleep, relieve anxiety, and even connect you with your own spiritual sense of being.

But first, you need to understand what your goals are. In a recent article on BlackDoctor.org, Dietician Constance Brown-Riggs suggests that over the age of fifty, your physical fitness goal should shift from weight maintenance to functional fitness as a primary. Functional fitness refers to exercises that "train your body for real situations," such as having enough endurance to traverse a flight of stairs, the strength for lifting your carry-on luggage on when you fly, or the flexibility and balance to keep yourself from tripping and falling on an uneven sidewalk (Brown-Riggs 2022). Maintaining functional fitness means you don't have to slow down your entire life because of sore joints. Nothing trashes self-esteem more than realizing that you can no longer do something as simple as walking to the end of the block without being out of breath.

But if you're like me and you're not into exercising, consider regimens that are alternatives to your typical trip to the gym.

- **Yoga and Tai Chi.** Yoga and Tai Chi check the boxes of building strength, flexibility, balance, *and* the added bonus of meditative techniques. Focusing on your breath can bring a sense of calm to your mind, which has a good chance of lowering your blood pressure and anxiety levels. You can also incorporate whatever your spiritual practice is. For instance, if prayer is therapeutic for you, try praying during your Yoga practice.

- **Dancing.** One of the things I first learned to do when I adopted my own exercise regimen was to "trick" my brain into thinking I was doing something other than exercise. Since I loved dancing, I found that to be the quickest way to get my body moving. From hustle classes to salsa, dancing can help improve coordination and brain function. It can also connect your higher mind to your physical one, as dancing and music can be spiritual and uplifting in practice.

- **Exercise with a group.** This is pretty simple. Working out with a partner or a friend or two can keep you motivated. It's a lot harder to skip a workout when your girlfriends are counting on you to show up at the gym or Yoga class. Whatever you decide to do, I promise you, exercising with someone else increases your chances of sticking to it.

- **Get creative.** So, sometimes, just getting there keeps you from your fitness goals. In fighting the idea that you're getting older, you might tend to steer away from exercises that your mother or grandmother did back in the day. Speed walking through the mall in the early morning hours might be good exercise, but if you're like me, you're probably looking for something more fun. Open your mind to alternative activities such as belly dancing (good for strength, flexibility, coordination, and self-esteem) or paddle board Yoga (good for balance and flexibility, though it should be done in a bathing suit as you will be standing above the water). Whatever you do, keep it fun. Enjoying what you're doing will make you look forward to it instead of dreading it.

The Divinity of your Temple

As I said earlier, I define my body as a temple. I care for it outwardly, and I foster the spirit within. Caring for myself is a part of honoring the divine feminine force within me and connecting it with the divine force all around us. When you find your spiritual path and connect with it, it shows. It's no different than keeping my house clean or decorating my front door. When the world sees me, I give them the best impression of my higher self before I even open my mouth because the spirit around me is joined with my personal life force.

This is a tough one for a lot of us these days. Many in our generation are undergoing the process of deconstructing the spiritual and religious practices of our upbringing. But we have to understand that religion and spirituality are not one and the same. Even if you no longer prescribe to a particular religion, that doesn't mean you're cut off from a righteous path. It just means that your journey won't necessarily be the same as those around you and, honestly, that's how it's supposed to be. Your path to the divine is yours and yours alone. However, once you find that path, however, you'll notice a change that everyone around you can see.

- **You've got to pray just to make it today.** Okay, so that was kind of corny, but hear me out. Prayer can actually help with anxiety and provide calm within you. Did you know that alcoholics in recovery are often encouraged to seek out a higher power? Not because recovery specialists are pious people but because the act of releasing your worry into something bigger than yourself can literally lift emotional weight from your shoulders. If you're not particularly religious, that doesn't mean you can't subscribe to the idea of letting go and letting God. It's not about religion but about relinquishing control of the things you can't control or do not serve you.

- **Be like water.** In addition to being the baddest thing walking and talking, Bruce Lee was a philosopher. He applied many of his philosophical teachings through martial arts. How does knowing this information help you? Am I telling you to sign up for Kung Fu classes? Well, kind of. See, martial arts have the added benefit of teaching patience and stillness of spirit. If you don't kick like you used to, consider more fluid practices like Tai Chi or Qigong. While not as exciting to watch, it's a great way to ease the spirit within you.

- **Take a deep breath and listen.** This practice can be applied to everything in life, but for yourself, take a moment out of every day and listen to your environment. You can be in a quiet spot or waiting for the train on your way to work. Wherever you are, take about five or ten minutes to just listen. Listen to your inner voice and the ticking of the clock on the wall. Just stop and be still for a few moments a day. This practice aligns with learning mindfulness and meditation (which we'll cover later), but starting with just this will get you in tune with your spirit and the rhythm of your environment.

Tanya's Hair

I have a friend who I've known since I was in high school. When we were teenagers, she was considered one of the most beautiful girls in school. With her thick, long hair that went down her back, she turned the head of every boy in our school and drew the ire of a few girls who thought her hair was a weave. See, if you remember, back in the eighties and nineties, there was this myth that black girls couldn't have long hair on their own.

Tanya's long hair was more of a product of her genetics than any degree of care she put into it. Like the rest of us, she labored until the false belief that wearing your hair naturally was unsightly and undignified. So, she lived in relaxers, redoing her roots every month at the salon, making sure it stayed bone straight, even in the dampest of rainy days.

Tanya and I eventually grew up, and while we ended up on different parts of the country for college, we still kept in touch over the years. Our conversations would sometimes turn to the subject of her hair. Like clockwork, she kept it long and relaxed.

Around her fiftieth birthday, I decided to pay her a visit in New York, where she lived. I'd never been there before and was eager to check out the Broadway shows and try some authentic New York cuisine. When my plane landed, I almost passed her up at the airport. Tanya's long, thick hair was short, natural, and completely silver! I couldn't believe what I was seeing. She'd completely changed her look...and she looked fantastic. What's more, there was a light in her eyes that was new. She seemed to glow on her own light.

Later, as we ate lunch, I asked what her secret was. She smiled and told me the story of how she discovered her true self. It started when she made her monthly trip to the salon. Her hair had been getting thinner and there was a lot of breakage going on. She'd gone to her hairdresser for help, but there wasn't much to be done. Her advancing age and years of chemical damage to her hair had taken its toll. The only solution was to cut it all off and start over.

For Tanya, her hair was more than just about the length and texture. It represented her place in the community, how she viewed herself, and her youth. Cutting it was a traumatic experience, and she felt like she no longer had any of those attributes. Now, she was not only bald but truly *old*. (There's that word again!) Tanya mourned her hair for weeks, refusing to be seen without a hat or a scarf on her head. She even debated wearing wigs for a little while there.

It wasn't until she went to visit her mother, who gave her the most important advice she'd ever learned. "Your hair isn't you. It's just how you decorate you, that's all. Think of your hair as an adornment instead of your identity. I say that it's just time for new decorations."

It was so simple, but the change in perspective had a profound effect on Tanya. She started turning her focus away from the hair she lost and to what she did have. Short, salt and pepper curls. She decided she was going to celebrate what was left behind. And it didn't stop at her hair. She started traveling and exploring new adventures. She even took up pole dancing to get herself into shape.

That was five years ago. At fifty-five now, she's turned her silver hair into long braids, and she changed pole dancing to salsa. But she feels more comfortable in her own skin, and all it took was defining what makes her temple. Her spirit shines through in a way that it never did before.

CHAPTER TWO

Temple Repair

"Communities and countries and
ultimately the world are only as strong
as the health of their women"

— *Michelle Obama*

Cracks in the Foundation

You know how you used to be able to dance a certain way and then one day, you just couldn't? Or how you used to be able to eat whatever you wanted, with absolutely no consequences at all? Yeah, those were the good old days, weren't they? I think we all want to go back to a time when we didn't have to worry about things like high blood pressure and arthritis and all that. Nothing hurts worse, I think, than the day you go in for a check-up and you find out your body has started tapping out before you're ready for it.

The reality of life is that eventually, you will have to deal with chronic conditions, illnesses, or even injuries directly related to your advancing age. If you're lucky, you'll encounter changes gradually, but sometimes, reality just comes along and slaps you across the face. Either way, the time will come for all of us to face challenges, a lot of which can be unique to us as black women.

According to the CDC, the second leading cause of death in black women 45-64 years of age is heart disease (Centers for Disease Control and Prevention 2016) and there are a lot of reasons behind that. Heart disease can be genetic within black families and that, coupled with poor diet and exercise habits, can lead down a bad road quicker than you might think. But that's the textbook reason heart disease is so prevalent among black women of our age.

Consider many environmental factors. What am I talking about? Outside of the stress of carrying so much on our backs, there are certain myths and disparities within the medical community about us that can be directly linked to our cause of death. Within the last ten to fifteen years, several studies surrounding pain management and clinicians treating black women uncovered rampant racial bias (Hoffman, et al. 2016). Apparently, an extremely antiquated idea that black women don't feel pain nearly as much as white women still thrives within the medical community. Under the guideline that black women don't feel pain the same way, a black woman complaining of chest pain in the ER may be dismissed and sent home if the doctor doesn't believe her about the degree of pain.

And that leads to mistrust within the black community when it comes to healthcare, which, in turn, leads to fewer trips to the doctor, especially once we're up in age. It doesn't have to be that way, though. And in fact, things are changing, albeit very slowly. Still, always remember to look out for yourself when you're getting care. Navigating your medical needs is important, and you should never ignore the cracks in your temple.

The Unavoidable

While diet and exercise can help ease complications with minor conditions, sometimes you just have to bite the bullet and see a professional for whatever is ailing you. So, let's talk about the elephant in the room when it comes to the most common condition. That's right. I'm talking about the dreaded menopause.

Have you ever seen that episode of *The Cosby Show* where Clair goes through menopause and her kids have all these insane notions about what she must be going through? They make it seem like she's suddenly going to turn into this raving maniac at the stroke of twelve. Even though we live in the information age and everything that you could possibly want to know about menopause is right at our fingertips, I'm willing to bet that you've already got some wild ideas in your mind about what you're in for.

I mean, we all know a friend of a cousin who had hot flashes so bad that she had to sit in a tub of ice water for a month or some other such nonsense. Everybody has ideas about what we think menopause is, whether it's a time for celebration or tragedy. Personally, I've always heard terrible opinions about it and listening to those opinions struck a chord of fear within me before I had to go through it. I didn't know what to expect or even when to expect it. Two of the myths that I believed was that menopause happened around your late fifties to sixties, and once it did, like the clock striking midnight at the end of Cinderella, I was going to turn into an irritable, sweaty mess. Imagine my surprise when menopause greeted me at fifty and I was still the same person I was before I was diagnosed.

The misinformation I received came from the fact that I'd never really discussed it with my doctor beyond whether or not it had occurred yet. I didn't ask any questions because I was convinced of the myths that I'd been told. I know that sounds terrible, but I honestly think that's how most of us approach it. We feel like the experience will be the same as our mothers and our mother's mothers. I'm here to tell you that nothing could be further from the truth.

First of all, you'd be interested to know that menopausal symptoms can begin at any time, starting from the age of forty-five. *Forty-five.* The transition from perimenopausal to full-on menopause usually takes about seven years but can go on for as long as fourteen (National Institute on Aging 2021). Now, don't let that freak you out because all that means is that your body is regulating itself for the next phase of your life. It is unlikely that you'll just wake up one morning a sweaty monster. You will more than likely start seeing signs of it well before then.

When I found out just this part of the equation, it blew me away, and it got me thinking about everything I thought I knew about conditions that could affect me. I started asking more questions, and suddenly, I was way more involved in my own healthcare and management. This shift in my thinking has helped me manage conditions that could have been more severe, such as osteoarthritis and high blood pressure—both conditions that are manageable with a doctor's care.

I'm saying all this to tell you that finding out is better than not knowing. But if you're unconvinced and you're willing to do a little research, here are a few thoughts:

- **The internet**. So, here's the thing. The internet is a fabulous resource for anything you might want to find out, except when it's not. What do I mean by that? Well, the internet has the answers you're looking for, but not the wisdom you'll need to understand it. Yes, those symptoms could be something serious, but doctors usually have to weigh symptoms against your history and testing before they can determine what's going on with you, and if you don't know how to do that, seeing symptoms on a page can lead you to believe you're having a stroke, when all you're actually having is a migraine. All I'm saying is take what you find with a grain of salt and discuss it with your doctor.

- **There's a reason they're called silent killers.** Getting a diagnosis like high blood pressure and diabetes can be daunting. I can't tell you how many women I've known who were diagnosed with a manageable illness and chose not to manage them. I think it's because when you don't feel any different, you think that it can't be that bad. No matter what the doctors say. No matter what your blood tests say. You kind of get it in your head that you're fine and you don't need to take your meds *every* day. Well, let me tell you from the perspective of a woman who has watched friends and family die from making that choice. Get it right out of your head right now and take your meds. Think of it this way: If you follow your doctor's orders and you're wrong, what have you lost? Nothing? Then there's no reason not to do it. You'll thank me later.

- **Don't be afraid to ask.** Talking to your doctor about certain things like menopause can be embarrassing for some of us, but trust me, you'll feel better for doing it. Discussing your health with someone whose entire job is medicine is better than going off half-cocked about something. Talk. Listen. And take the advice you're given. But also, don't be afraid to question things you don't understand. It's better to get a full picture of your health than not, trust me.

A Few Good Doctors

I'm willing to bet you read all that above and you thought, "But how am I supposed to trust a doctor? I've got a friend/cousin/sister who trusted one and now she's (insert horrible fate here)."

Yeah, I get that. In fact, I *was* that at one point. And given that we just had a discussion about doctors and implicit bias, I get why you wouldn't trust them. I mean, I haven't spoken to every black woman in the world, but I'm willing to bet that most of, if not all, black women have had a negative experience with a doctor at one point in time in their life. After a certain age, the events may have happened so many times, and as you approach your later years, you may be reluctant to visit the doctor as regularly as you should. I'm not going to lie to you, I get why we've got every reason to worry. That doesn't mean we should ignore our health altogether, however.

That being said, I've found that it's not about ignoring all doctors. It's about finding the *right* doctor. But finding a doctor you can trust is difficult. What makes that a daunting task is the idea of going to doctor after doctor and not getting the results you want. Many of us stay with doctors who don't meet our needs because who wants to run around from office to office, jumping through the hoops of filling out paperwork and providing records to a new doctor over and over again?

Just the same, staying with a doctor who doesn't meet your needs defeats the purpose of seeing one in the first place. So, when looking for a new doctor, here are a few ways to stay on track with your own needs.

- **Review your medical records regularly.** Most doctor's offices have electronic medical records that you can access. If you prefer hard copies legally speaking, the doctor has to give you any copies of your records that you might request. While you're entitled to your records, keep in mind that the office can charge you a fee to obtain copies, so be prepared for that possibility. However, asking for a single copy of your latest blood work usually doesn't apply to records fees.

Knowing exactly what tests you've had will help with your treatment with a new doctor. The easier you make it for them, the better your relationship with your new doctor can be.

- **Recognize when you're not being heard.** There have been instances throughout my life where a doctor has disregarded something I've told him/her. In almost all those cases, the end result ended up prolonging the process of the treatment I needed. Doctors often deal with patients who want to diagnose themselves, and I get it. The patient doesn't know more than someone who studied medicine for most of their adult life. But that should not lead to a doctor who refuses to listen to legitimate concerns. Your doctor is here for you, not the other way around. If you suspect you're not being heard, consider finding a new physician.

- **Become your own advocate.** Putting all your trust in a physician is tough for some of us. So tough that we often don't speak up when we have questions or think we need testing. But you have to make your needs clear if you want them met. If you want a particular blood test, ask for it. If you have an embarrassing question, ask it. Your doctor is not a psychic, so let him in on everything that's going on with you.

- **Don't be afraid to leave if you have to.** I cannot stress this one enough! Let's get something straight. A visit to the doctor is about your care and your needs. If those needs aren't being met, then that doctor is not for you and the right to move on to a new doctor doesn't need explanation. If they're rude, incompetent, or you don't like their vibe, all reasons are valid if your needs are not being met.

- **Consider black doctors.** That might be a slightly controversial opinion, but when you consider the whole racial disparity gap in medicine, maybe it's just prudent to seek out a doctor who knows that disparity all too well. Don't choose solely on race, of course, but keep it top of mind. A black doctor will more likely know about and understand conditions that uniquely affect us and how ignoring them could cause bigger issues.

Ignore Those Cracks at Your Own Peril

When I think about heart disease being the second biggest killer of black women in my age range, you might wonder how that could be. Everyone knows the symptoms of a heart attack and would immediately seek medical attention. Surely, if we know that it runs in our families, we will resort to eating better and getting more exercise. And yet, that doesn't appear to be the case. While you can blame the medical community or our own dietary missteps for this statistic, you are missing one significant factor: we tend to ignore the symptoms.

Our society has us placed on a pedestal of strength. We are strong black women. We manage our families, our jobs, and our businesses. We take care of everyone in our lives before taking care of ourselves, and we do it with stoic strength. It's the one thing we are praised for in most cases.

Imagine being at your high-powered job for eight hours a day, sitting in traffic for an hour and a half on the way home, picking up your children, cooking dinner, cleaning the dishes, and suddenly experiencing chest pain and feeling nauseous. What do you do? I'm willing to bet all of you would ignore it and go on about your night.

Or let's say you're just sitting at home with your husband. You're retired and your life is fairly low stress, and all day you've been having chest and arm pains. Do you go to the doctor? You probably wouldn't.

Don't ignore your symptoms. Your body has the ability to give you more than enough warning against disaster, so listen to it when you start getting alarms. Keep an open communication with your doctor and stay on top of your health. Chances are you'll be the first person to see trouble coming, so don't ignore it. Do something about it.

Lashawn and the Headache

I have a story to share about a nurse I knew many moons ago named Lashawn. She worked as a receptionist in a doctor's office while in nursing school. One day, she got a call from a patient, Mrs. Jones, a fifty-seven-year-old black woman in reasonably good health. She called to schedule a regular check-up and to refill her medications. Lashawn made her an appointment.

The day of her appointment arrived and Lashawn noticed that Mrs. Jones seemed out of sorts. When Lashawn asked her about it, she told her she'd been having a headache for about a week. No big deal. She told her Lashawn she had been getting headaches like this off and on for a while and they always go away or she just forgets to mention it to the doctor. She promised to talk to the doctor about it when she sees her.

Following this, Mrs. Jones saw the doctor, but Lashawn found out later that she didn't actually mention it. Though Lashawn was a bit concerned, she let it go, hoping it was nothing serious. Within the next few days, Mrs. Jones called back, complaining of a terrible headache and requesting the doctor to call in some medication. Lashawn relayed the message to the doctor, who called in the medication.

This continued until one day, Mrs. Jones came in and one half of her face was drooping. When Lashawn pointed it out, Mrs. Jones was surprised. She had noticed the numbness on her way over but figured it would go away. The very next thing she said sent chills up Lashawn's spine.

Mrs. Jones suddenly began speaking in gibberish. Lashawn brought her back to see the doctor right away. Minutes later, an ambulance was called. Mrs. Jones was having a stroke.

Fortunately, Mrs. Jones survived the ordeal, though she lost all feeling on one side of her body and had to undergo extensive rehabilitation. It took her several months before she could walk again. When Lashawn recounts this story, she wonders about all the times that Mrs. Jones complained about a headache and never mentioned it to the doctor. If she'd gotten help sooner, she might've made a full recovery. This goes to show that your health is important enough to speak up about it, so remember to always advocate for yourself and maintain a good relationship with your doctor.

CHAPTER THREE

Top of Mind

"When I dare to be powerful, to use
my strength in the service of my
vision, then it becomes less and less
important whether I am afraid."

— Audre Lorde

Your Most Important Organ

Years ago, when my grandmother passed away,
my family and I were tasked with the duty of
clearing out her home and her belongings. She
had not left any will, which was fine since she didn't
have much of an estate, and it was my mother and her

brother as her next of kin. While we were clearing out her little rental apartment, my mother discovered stacks and stacks of old crossword and puzzle books in her bedroom. I remember seeing her with those books all the time as a child. She always seemed to have one stashed in her bag wherever she went.

Back then, I thought that was something that old ladies did. They did crossword and Sudoku puzzles because those were just "old people" things. (They're not, of course. But I was twelve at the time. What did I know?) And because I believed these old people things were strictly for old people, I didn't bother with them for the most part. I enjoyed doing crosswords with my grandmother, and I was quite good at word searches in school, but you'd never catch me with any of those books in my little backpack.

I found out later that my grandmother didn't play those scores and scores of puzzles just for fun. She played them because she knew they would keep her mind sharp in her later years, and she was one hundred percent correct. Numerous studies (including one big one from the National Library of Medicine) have concluded that mind puzzles such as crossword, word searches, and any variety of other similar games have proven to delay conditions such as dementia and Alzheimer's (Pillai, et al. 2014).

So, I told you all that because when we're talking about total self-care, I'd be remiss if I didn't say anything about how to take care of your mind, especially as a black woman. Studies have shown that black women are two to three times more likely to develop dementia and Alzheimer's than white women (Findley, et al. 2023). That sounds pretty scary, but just like my grandmother figured it out, you can too.

You may be thinking, "But you're only *fifty!* Do you really have to resort to crosswords?" Well, while puzzles are great for improving mental function, it's not the only game in town. Even if you're not showing any immediate signs of dementia just yet, that doesn't mean you can't start doing things now to improve your mental function. And why shouldn't those things be fun as well?

But Seriously for a Second

Before we dive into some ways to stave off the dreaded shadow of dementia, I thought you might be interested to know how serious this is for our community. One of the biggest issues that we have as a whole is...well, taking care of our mental health in general.

This was never more evident than when COVID hit America. So, never mind the fact that because of institutionalized racism, oppression, and trauma and about a dozen other reasons, black folks are not and have never been quick to go to a therapist. When COVID hit, mental health in the black community took a nosedive. The instability of our workplaces shutting down coupled with job loss sunk a lot of our spirits (Lockett 2023). Many older adults suffered mental distress due to isolation and lack of community.

The fact of the matter is that we don't have a very good history with healthcare in general. Seeking therapy, especially, is often viewed as admitting to being "crazy" or unstable within our community. But I've always believed it's the ones who don't get help who end up losing mental stability.

And the real tragedy is that, as a community, we largely suffered alone. But then, that's always been the case. As a result, social and religious groups within our communities stepped in to fill the gap. Still, it's pretty clear that therapists are sorely needed within the black community.

Oh, I just said a bad word, didn't I? Don't think I don't know some of you just cringed right now at the mere mention of therapy. Listen, when it comes to combating mental illness of any kind, the first line of defense is often your therapist. All jokes aside, your therapist will more than likely be the first one to see early signs of things like dementia and Alzheimer's and they will be the ones that can offer you solutions tailored to work for you. In short, a therapist's whole job is to help you manage your mental health. And in the end, they are the ones who will guide you through the rough times and help you back into the light.

Now. Back to our regularly scheduled programming with some tips on how you can work on keeping your mind sharp in the meantime.

Everybody Wants to Be in the Band

When I was younger, I think I did what most young people at least attempt to do once in their lives—I tried to learn how to play piano. At sixteen, I pictured myself playing for family weddings and showing off my skills at random parties. I always wanted to be the girl who could just sit down at the piano at a party and start playing some complicated classical piece.

And as you do when you're young, I lost interest pretty quickly. Every now and then, though, I wonder what it might've been like if I'd stuck with it. For a while, I just chalked it up to the folly of youth as I couldn't attach it to anything practical. I think we've all done that before.

But since we're talking about alternative ways to keep your mind sharp, have you ever considered learning an instrument? And no! It's not too late to learn! Get that out of your head right now. It's never too late to learn a new skill. Here are some stats and ideas that you can work with and try for yourself:

- **Dust off that old guitar in the corner.** Piano, guitar, drums, a hurdy-gurdy or a glass harmonica, it doesn't matter. Learning to play an instrument has been shown to be good for your memory and cognitive skills and has the double bonus of improving fine motor skills (Cowles, et al. 2003). Plus, you can be that cool grandma who can shred guitar.

- **Get to know your French neighbors.** One of the things I picked up in my older years was learning French, mostly because I've always wanted to go to Paris. I always imagined how embarrassing it would be to get all the way to France, only to be the only one unable to speak the language. But learning another language has more benefits than being able to order food in an Italian restaurant. Bilingual people have better focus, memory, visual-spatial skills, and higher executive function than monolingual people (Mendez 2019). So, pick a language and get to learning.

- **Live the author life.** Okay, I might be a little biased with this one, but upping your writing skills can not only improve your cognitive function but can also give you something that can add to your legacy. And when I say live the author life, I don't necessarily mean go out and write and publish a novel (though, if you'd like to, who am I to stop you). Keep a diary, make it into a scrapbook, and add pictures to it. Write down your family history. Write a story strictly from your imagination just for the fun of it.

- **Dance like nobody's watching**. Dancing doesn't just improve your body, but it helps your memory too. Consider choreography. The more you start to learn choreography, the better your memory will get. It turns out it's a muscle memory thing for your muscles and your brain.

Off the Beaten Path

So, let's say you're the kind of woman who doesn't really follow the beat of anyone else's drum. You shaved your head in the summer, and you wear wild-colored wigs in the winter. You may have a tattoo or three and maybe even a piercing. You are not the typical fifty-plus woman. You listen to 90s hip hop or rock music at extremely high volumes in your car and you still rock that ankh necklace that you bought at the African Festival back in '92.

Statistically speaking, I'm probably addressing more black women like you than even I could have expected. It's the modern age and the black "round-the-way" girl from 1993 is either coming up in her fifties pretty soon or has already celebrated the big milestone of her life. If you fit into this category, you're probably not going to hustle classes for exercise and you're definitely not doing any crossword puzzles either. But that doesn't mean you're not looking to preserve some of your brain cells as well.

For you, I would consider the alternate routes of brain exercise, of which there are many. You just have to open your mind a little. But that probably won't be a problem for you, will it?

- *Mario Kart* **is not just for kids anymore.** Okay, hear me out. I am aware that playing video games carries a particular stigma. If you're not already playing the latest *Final Fantasy* game and you've been turning your nose up at the whole idea of picking up a controller, consider the fact that playing video games actually improves cognitive function and memory loss. No, really. It does. In fact, one study showed that people aged 60 to 80 who played video games every day over the course of a month scored higher on memory tests by the end of the month (Clemenson 2020). Done in moderation, you can actually improve your brain function considerably by being a gamer. I know, I know. It's wild. But go on ahead and get that PS5 for the den. I promise I won't tell your kids.

- **Find your *Jeopardy* game**. There's an old episode of *Blossom* where Joey (played by Joey Lawrence) writes all the answers to a test down all over his body in order to cheat. He spends all night doing this and, on the day of the exam, finds that he's accidentally memorized the answers and, therefore, doesn't have to cheat for the test. That's kind of how getting into trivia works. The more you play trivia games, the more your brain remembers the information. The more you encourage your brain to do that, the better your memory will be. So, join a game of *Jeopardy* or attend a Trivia Crack Game in your local community center on Wednesdays. Whatever you do, make sure to encourage your brain to retain information.

- **Circus performers probably have great memories.** So, again, here me out, here. I'm not telling you to try axe throwing or lion taming (though if you do, I can't really speak to any cognitive benefits), but there are a few things you can learn that you might only see in the circus. Such as contact juggling or trapeze and aerial acrobatics. All of which can be beneficial for your hand-eye coordination, memory, and cognitive function. Just be safe out there. I don't want to hear about any high-wire acts going wrong.

Caring for Your Crown Chakra

This book wouldn't be complete without mentioning your spiritual connection in all this. Regardless of your religious affiliation, understanding that if you have a peaceful mindset, your mind will have a chance to grow and heal is extremely important. That being said, I know that many of you might reject the idea of meditation as a form of therapy for your mind.

You have to understand that meditation *can* be connected to a religious or spiritual practice, but it doesn't necessarily have to be. Some forms of meditation have no true connection to any religious doctrine if you have concerns about opening yourself up to evil spirits or demonic energies. Meditation in it itself is just a way for you to calm the storm inside your mind, which all of us have experienced from time to time.

Meditation has been proven to improve focus and calm anxiety with statistical evidence. It has been implemented in schools, convalescent care homes, and even prisons. Practitioners have marked significant improvements in their mental health as well as physical health from long-term practice. Here's a short list of some different types of meditation you could get connected to.

- **Guided Meditation.** This type of meditation is probably the most common that you've heard of. You might have heard of guided meditation tapes from the '90s that you could pop into your Walkman and listen to while you ride the subway to work. All it means is that someone is "guiding" you through visualizing calm and serene surroundings.

- **Mindfulness Meditation.** This type of meditation is a lot like guided meditation in that you can visualize a serene surrounding, but the goal here is to focus on your breathing and listening to your surroundings. The goal of mindfulness is to experience being "here now." It's a way to connect with your thoughts and emotions, something we often tend to forget about until they sneak up on us.

- **Transcendental Meditation.** Okay, so stay with me here. This one is the only one on this list that requires a teacher for the first session but can be done anywhere after that. Basically, you're given a mantra. The mantra can be a word or a phrase. You will repeat that mantra in your mind over and over for twenty minutes, twice a day. I realize how oddly specific that one sounds, but TM practitioners have reported achieving focus and has the added bonus of helping with PTSD and other traumatic experiences (Mayer 2022).

- **Yoga Meditation.** This type of meditation uses Yoga poses and focuses on your breathing to calm your mind. The great thing about Yoga meditation is that it's a way to connect your body, your mind, *and* your spirit. It's an all-purpose kind of meditation.

Punk Metal Gramma

During the '80s, Angela was a tattoo artist at a local parlor in her town. The establishment was one of the first places in her city that specialized in tattoos for black skin, and she was proud of her work. A natural artist, Angela designed all her own artwork, and by the '90s, she'd built up a large list of clients from her detailed work.

Angela lived a good life and earned a good living as a tattoo artist. She also had a very unconventional life. Covered in tattoos and a few piercings, she was considered "alternative" before anyone called it that and she loved it. She loved being as different as possible.

When the 2000s rolled around, Angela was aging, but she was still the same person inside that she'd always been. Sure, her knees got a little creakier and she now had to take medication to keep her blood pressure down, but that didn't mean you still didn't see her out on her porch in the morning, sipping her tea while wearing her Misfits T-shirt and sporting dreaded hair. Inside, Angela was as "alternative" as she'd always been.

One day, Angela decided to pick up an instrument. For no other reason than that she never had the time before to learn. She chose electric guitar and started slow, learning all the chords and old songs from songbooks she borrowed from the library. She kept up the practice for a while, then switched to bass guitar. When she got bored of that, she started learning Spanish.

Now that she has retired from tattooing, she wanted to keep her mind fresh. She never saw herself as being old and decrepit. She wanted to stave off any age-related concerns as much as possible. Today, you can find Angela playing chess in Central Park. She's sharp-tongued and funny. She can tell you amazing stories from her childhood and her ex-husbands (two of them as I recall), and she knows where the best pizza in town is made. She also just had her eighty-fifth birthday. When I asked Angela what her secret was to staying so mentally sharp, she said, "I never stopped learning, even when people told me that I should sit down somewhere."

So, keep building your skills. Keep learning and your brain will thank you for it.

PART TWO

Community and Relationships

CHAPTER FOUR

Finding your People

> "The times may have changed, but the people are still the same. We're still looking for love, and that will always be our struggle as human beings."
>
> —Halle Berry

Your People and How to Find Them

I t's been my experience that the definition of who your "people" are can change over the years. Traditionally, as black people, we've defined our "people" as our family. It's an old term that the elders used to use when I was young, as in, "Who's your people? You're the Johnson girl, right?" But in later years, I've heard the term refer to not only family but friends and found family. Your people are the ones who you depend on and confide in. They are the ones who you call in the middle of the night with your worries. They're your girlfriends and boyfriends. They're your cousins and play cousins. They're your *people*.

Who our people are can change over time. As we grow out of our teens and go off to college, we might meet new people who better define who we're becoming. After we grow out of our twenties, work friendships form as we find ourselves growing out of the bonds of college life. Not to mention how many social and political shifts have happened in the last twenty years or so that have maybe caused you to change your mind about the company you keep. The point is, it's not uncommon to hit your fifties, and suddenly find your friendships have changed or possibly disappeared completely.

Sometimes it's tougher when you're older to find the tribe that fits who you are now. Back then, you could make a gang of friends at the club or maybe at your job at the restaurant. Now, you may be retired. Your children may be adults, so there's no PTA to join. Your life is entirely different, and now you've got to make new friends. Never fear, though. It's still pretty easy to find your community.

No, Being a Hermit Isn't an Option

The funny thing about having an empty nest is that it's only aggravating at *first*. Trying to find your new normal now that your kids have grown up and moved out or perhaps now that your significant other has passed on can be a frightening and frustrating experience. But eventually, you'll look up and realize that not only are you fine...but you're actually pretty great.

Think about it. Now you can get up in the morning without worrying about getting anyone else up for work or school. You can leave the house and go wherever you want at any time of day without putting anyone in a car seat. You've achieved a certain degree of freedom in your solitude. That's good, right?

Well, it can be. But it can also hurt you in some significant ways including coronary health and mental decline. Being alone can lead to loneliness. Through loneliness, depression can manifest, which can bring about bad eating and exercise habits that can raise your risk of heart disease and several other related diseases. Everything within our bodies is connected and when we're out of balance, the negative effects fall on our bodies like dominoes.

That being said, connecting with a community can help keep you healthy in multiple ways. Let's have a look at a few benefits of connecting with a community.

- **Your own personal cheer team.** It can be hard to stay motivated when you're on your own, but being part of a community means you have your own cheer squad. My grandmother used to be a part of a bowling team that not only competed but they leaned on each other for support or improvement in their skills. The end result was a solid team that started winning a few trophies. And nothing feels better than winning as a team.

- **Networking.** Personally, I don't like the word networking. It makes it seem like you'll be handing out business cards at a convention center. That being said, the fundamentals of networking are just creating connections and contacts, which you should consider. The thing is, having a solid network of friends means you can achieve more things outside your newfound community should you need to. For instance, that Beyonce concert you've been dying to go to? Maybe someone in your swim club is looking to unload some tickets. You'll never know until you connect with them.

- **Inspiration and creativity.** Many years ago, my mother decided to take an art class. She'd never painted a day in her life, but she thought it might be fun to learn how to create artwork for her house. Admittedly, she never became very good at it. However, meeting other creative minds opened her mind to new ideas in other aspects of her life. For instance, she befriended a woman who happened to be an excellent cook. The two of them got together and started exchanging recipes, each dish more gourmet than the last. I think my father gained at least ten pounds in the time that they connected, but my mother found herself inspired just by cooking with her new friend.

- **Social revenue.** I feel a little like this is a no-brainer. Being a part of a club or a community means you get to socialize with different people, but it can also mean you have the chance to discover people from backgrounds different than yours. Finding a group that has a diverse population can broaden your world in ways you never thought possible. You'll gain empathy and compassion, and you might learn something new.

Community Property Values

Now comes the tricky part of finding your people...and that's finding your people. You might think there are a lot of places out there that are a perfect fit for you before you even arrive, but you'd be surprised at what appears to be right for you and what actually *is* right for you.

For example, I've known several women in my personal friend group who at one point in time or another found themselves looking for a new church home. And the reasons were varied. Some found the doctrine too strict and unyielding, while one of them couldn't stand the way the congregation had a tendency to gossip. For others, it was because they didn't like the Pastor or Bishop and sometimes, or because they moved to another city or state. Regardless of the reason, every single one of them went into the search with the idea that they were going to find their people at their new church home. Some of them did, but others were disappointed and had to start searching again.

My point is that every one of them was *sure* that they would find community within their new churches. To their credit, none of them gave up their search, but I can tell you that a few of them ended up changing denominations before they found a church home they were comfortable with. What worked for them was opening their minds to different possibilities within their faiths. You can apply that same philosophy when looking for your own people, not just in church, but in any social activity.

- **Want to keep in shape? Consider classes at the community center**. Now, I say a community center instead of a gym because you can find a variety of different physical activities that may suit you. If you like to swim, dance, or just exercise, you'll be able to find classes there that you can connect with.

- **Bob Ross had the right idea**. One of the things I loved about Bob Ross was that he took a medium like painting and turned it into something anyone can do. His program on PBS ran throughout the '80s and millions of people tuned in to learn how to create beautiful landscapes with the simplest of techniques. If you're thinking that you might want to learn to paint, sure, classes would work fine, but maybe it's more about having fun and connecting with people rather than the painting itself. Consider places like Painting with a Twist, a company that offers painting lessons along with cocktails (or mocktails for those who don't drink) for the guests attending. The activity was more about having fun rather than learning to paint, but you're liable to get both in return.

- **Social media has a ton of communities.** Since the pandemic, many people are still having issues with going out and meeting people in public and I won't judge you if you're one of those people. Those two years indoors were hard for most people and trying to assimilate back into society might be difficult for you, even today. But that's where social media is handy. Outlets like Facebook Groups and Meetup have hundreds of groups that meet exclusively online and through video chat functions, which is a way to connect with others without the pressure of in-person interaction. These online options were available during the pandemic and will be there for anyone who still has social anxiety.

- **Clubs for the daring**. So, for those of you who are looking for something a little more exciting, believe it or not, there are motorcycle clubs for black women. I kid you not. The most famous of them is called Caramel Curves out of New Orleans (ABC News 2019). For those of you who have watched too many episodes of *Mayans M.C.*, let me be clear. I'm not talking about outlaw clubs or anything like that. These are, indeed, social clubs. They are black women who ride motorcycles stylishly. They wear the latest fashion trends and have custom bikes, and they come in all shapes, sizes, and ages. If you're a woman who rides, know that many other women out there do too.

Finding Peace at your Place of Worship

As I mentioned before, sometimes finding your people means finding the right place of worship for yourself. Within the black community, having a place to worship is a part of our culture. It doesn't matter what denomination or faith you belong to. Every black woman of faith has a similar experience of being connected with a place of worship from when we were children. And some of us haven't had the best experiences.

Finding your house of worship can be a taxing task, but I wouldn't give up on it entirely. The key is truly about connecting with a place that is your speed and is comfortable for you. I'm sure I don't have to tell any of you that spirituality and worship are serious things in our lives. So, it's important that we find the right place for us.

- **If it doesn't feel right, it's not for you**. This is a tough one to deal with, but it's important. Your path in connecting to the divine is your own. Write that down. *Your path in connecting to the* *divine is your own.* That means that if you're not getting your spiritual needs met, don't waste your time. If the minister preaches something that you don't agree with and you feel alienated for asking questions, maybe that's not the right place of worship for you.

- **Remember why you're there.** I think it's pretty easy to get caught up in superficial things when it comes to finding a church home. Maybe you're looking at whether it's a large congregation or if the building is in a good part of town. Or maybe the spiritual leader is handsome and easy to look at or talk to. Or maybe you just like the fact that they serve actual wine for communion. All of these things can be factors in your decision, but remember the real reason you're there is to connect with the divine and find your peace.

- **The congregation is as important as the church.** I know a lot of people who left the places of worship that they grew up in for new places they found as adults. It's not terribly uncommon, and the most common reason had to do with the congregation. While there are plenty of more nefarious reasons that I could list, honestly, a lot of people just want to start fresh somewhere where most of the people don't know them since they were young. Whatever the reason, if you can't get along with your neighbor, worshipping will be difficult. Pick a place where you feel like you belong within the congregation.

It's All About Finding Yourself

The day that Laura's husband passed, she felt like she had lost her best friend. The week after that, she realized she was all alone in their little three-bedroom house. Laura had two children. Both were grown and moved out. And now that her hubby was gone, it was just her and her cat George.

At first, Laura thought that everything would be fine. She would adjust her schedule and get used to living alone, just as anyone would. People go through this every day, she thought. She was no different than any other widow, after all. She would adjust.

But the days turned into weeks, and the weeks turned into months, and pretty soon a year had passed, and she was miserable. She'd gained twenty pounds from eating out instead of cooking for herself (since she was used to cooking for someone else as well). Her health was declining and her mental health was also taking a hit, as depression started to set in.

At the worst times, Laura was ready to give up. She truly felt she had no one in her life and she started to think she might be ready to join her dear husband on the other side. One day, while sitting outside, she noticed a crow in her garden. She chased it off, thinking that she needed to get something to keep them at bay.

The next day, when she went to the garden, she found coins scattered throughout the dirt and vegetables. She thought it was odd, but she picked them up anyway and put them in a jar. The following day, the same thing, only now she found other items as well. It was very, *very* odd. And every now and then, she'd catch a crow in her yard.

Laura went online to research the crows and discovered that crows leave gifts to humans they want to befriend. It seemed like a ridiculous idea, but she was fascinated in finding out more, so she put up a question about it on Reddit. She got hundreds of responses as to how to befriend the crows back and the benefits of having them as a part of her garden. She also got a message from someone asking if she'd like to join their online bird-watching group.

Feeling like she had nothing to lose, Laura joined the group. She found herself making friends fast online and with the crows in her garden. Today, Laura's backyard has become a sort of bird haven. She's since built a couple of birdhouses she keeps for all the birds that come in her yard, both of which she's been so proud of that she started a Pinterest page dedicated to them.

Her friends sometimes visit and help out, and they bird-watch together in the park. Laura went from being alone to having more friends than she knew what to do with and it was all because she took a chance and found her people.

CHAPTER FIVE

Searching for a Soulmate

"I have learned not to worry about love,
but to honor its coming with all my
heart."

– Alice Walker

Walking the World Alone

Okay, so that title might sound a bit dramatic, but let's be completely real for a moment about being single after fifty. Being single can feel much more intense than it actually is. Most of us in this generation have grown up with the idea that, as women, our lifelong goals have to include meeting someone, getting married, and having children. In our twenties, a lot of us centered our lives around this concept. Some of us even made it our entire personalities.

Now, I'm not putting you down if that's what you want in life. Black women belonging to the Gen X and Boomer generations have been raised to "be fruitful and multiply." It's a concept that has been preached to us from the pulpits and ingrained in our movies and music that we, as women, must find someone to grow old and die with. And if I'm being honest, that's not a bad thing to aspire to. Finding someone to love and to share a life and children with can be a wonderful and life-changing experience. In the best possible way, finding the love of your life can improve your physical and mental health exponentially. No, seriously. Statistically speaking, married couples tend to live longer. Research has shown that when you're married, you have a better chance of surviving acute diseases such as cancer and coronary dysfunction as well as more latent disorders such as dementia (Wiley 2016). Suffice it to say, we're talking about happy marriages here. The opposite is true in bad marriage situations.

And that being said, sometimes the married life just isn't in the plan for many of us. The reality is spouses don't always stick around. In the United States, black women have the highest divorce rate as of 2018 at 38.9%, with the highest group being Baby Boomers at 34.9% (Schweizer 2019). And sometimes, it's not as simple as circumstances leading to divorce. Sometimes, heaven forbid, it's death that leaves us without our loved ones.

But regardless of the circumstances, a lot of us are out here walking out into a dating world that is totally different from the one we left behind. At the risk of pulling a "back in my day" narrative, I can't remember the last time I heard of anyone meeting at a bar or a cabaret event. The world we live in is constantly changing, and because of that, the way we move has changed too.

Getting a Lay of the Land

I first started dating the way that most of us do—in high school. My parents did not allow me to date until I was around sixteen. I had a curfew and my father had to meet the boy before I would be allowed to go out with him. Teenage dating was easy. You met in school, you liked each other, you went out a few times, and became steady. Minus any teen drama that might occur, it's fairly textbook.

Now, when I hit my twenties, the internet was still very young. If you had a home computer, you were a tech-savvy kind of person who probably worked with them or had a vested interest in using them, you may have connected to other people through the earlier incarnations of chat boards and matchmaker sites (called BBS or Bulletin Board Systems). While I'm sure many people had success meeting their future spouses in places like this in the past, I'm willing to bet the majority of black women my age met their mates in much more traditional ways such as bars, church, or even phone chat lines (remember those?).

It was all very analog back then, but we got it done. If you've managed to stay with the person you met back then through all these years and now you're single, you're probably wondering how in the world you are ever going to navigate dating in this shiny new high-tech community? Well, the first thing is having some understanding of what's out there.

- **The internet marketplace.** So, I'm going to keep it one hundred with you. Internet dating is scary. And only about 20% of all adults over the age of fifty are even doing it at all (Vogels and McClain 2023). But suppose you decide to go this route. In that case, there are dozens of sites tailored especially for black women over the age of fifty (Silver Singles and Our Time are high-quality sites in particular). Or, really, *anyone* over the age of fifty. But I would caution you to educate yourself before diving into cyberspace. There are lots of people out there looking to take advantage of women for a variety of different reasons. The AARP has a fantastic article on dating scams in cyberspace and plenty of tips on how to keep yourself safe (AARP 2018).

- **Analog is still a thing, though.** Remember when I talked about getting out there and getting engaged with your community in the last chapter? Well, one benefit of doing that can be finding someone to date. Now, I wouldn't advise signing up for a book club, for example, for the sole purpose of hooking up. *However*, when you put yourself around people with similar interests to yours, you're more likely to mess around and find somebody you might want to date that has the added bonus of being into the same things you're into. Yes, high-tech dating is a thing, but meeting people the old-fashioned way is still available. When you connect in a place where you have a common interest, the battle's already won.

- **Don't count out charity work.** Fun fact—this was one of the ways that Prince Harry and Meghan Markle connected when they were dating. Prior to meeting Harry, Meghan Markle was already big on charity work for organizations in other countries (such as Africa) as a personal passion. And Harry, historically speaking, had spent a good chunk of his youth in Africa with his father and on other charitable ventures. I'm sure there are a bunch of other inexplicable connections that they made as a couple, but finding out they had the same love for making a better world had to be a bonus for both of them. But that's the great thing about meeting someone while volunteering. It mixes a common interest with your personal value system. When looking for a partner, it's important to find someone who shares your values and beliefs. And what better way to meet the one who will share this next chapter with you than to do it while doing something charitable?

Be Real with Your Expectations

For a lot of us, just getting back in the dating game, the act of being real with yourself can make all the difference.

For a lot of us, this is a hard sell because, at our age, we already have an idea of who we think we are. And in a lot of ways, we're absolutely on it. There's a reason why women of a certain age are considered more mature physically, mentally, and spiritually—for the most part, we are. We are the elders of the younger generation, which is something to be proud of. And it's something we should revel in.

Many times, when we find ourselves back in the dating pool, we forget that. We want to go back to how it was when we were young and naïve. We want that feeling of our savior riding in on a white horse and sweeping us away and into the night. We haven't been in the dating world for a minute, so we start doing things that we did in our twenties, thinking that this will work just as well as it did the last time.

Well, it's a new game and we're new women and how we date needs to reflect that. Our needs and preferences evolve with time, and what we looked for in a partner now may differ from what we looked for in our youth. If you're a list maker like me, at one point in time, you probably wrote down all the qualities you thought you needed in a perfect relationship. Now that you're older, how many of those things are the same? How many are different? How many don't even matter?

Give yourself a gut check and get real with who you are and what makes you happy in a relationship by setting realistic goals for yourself. Consider the following things:

- **Stay your behind out of Forever 21.** Don't take this as an indictment, meaning to act your age. Personally, I feel like that's an outdated concept anyway. If you feel younger than you are, well, then you'll automatically act younger. But there's a difference between acting young and *believing* you are younger than you are. It's the idea of shopping at Forever 21 even though the style of clothes doesn't suit who you are now. Get comfortable in your skin as a mature woman. Accept those stretch marks as scars that tell the stories behind your children or your weight loss or weight gain. Rejoice in your stiff joints knowing that they're stiff because you kept it moving. See you for you, warts and all. And why? Because confidence is the ultimate aphrodisiac. It attracts like bees to honey. It glows and people are automatically drawn to it. So get into being in love with yourself and everything that entails.

- **Understand the difference between Aloneness and Loneliness.** How many times have you heard someone referring to dying alone as being the worst thing that can happen to you? Here's a news flash. It's not. Many of us have ended up in relationships because we were afraid we would "die alone" and when the relationship doesn't work out, we scratch our heads and wonder why it failed. Recognize that being alone and being lonely are two completely different things. You don't have to accept loneliness, but if you don't know how to be alone, then you run the risk of letting someone else define your state of being. Do yourself a favor and get used to the concept that you are enough. Your partner should be your *partner*. Not your savior (or at least not solely your savior).

- **Throw the lists/vision boards away.** I have a friend who made a vision board a year ago. On said board, she put that she wanted to be married by the following year. At the time, she didn't even have a boyfriend, but she became so hyperfocused on being married that she completely disregarded a lot of important things about relationships. Lists and Vision Boards can be handy tools for manifesting such things as financial success or job opportunities, but they are just not good gameplans when it comes to human relations. As humans, we are messy, complicated, and imperfect. You have no hope of trying to control the path of another human being's direction toward you no matter how you try, so don't. Accept who comes into your life and evaluate them on realistic expectations. Sure, magical connections happen all the time and good for you if you meet the perfect person by way of kismet, but most of the time, the connections you make are more logical than you think, so take off the rose-tinted glasses and get real.

- **Compliment, not complete.** If there's one thing I can't stand, it's when somebody says something to the effect of "Well, at least I got somebody." Especially since, most of the time, that alone is not the flex you think it is. We all want to be in a loving relationship, but you need to have the firm understanding that being happy and being alone always trumps being with someone who makes you feel alone. You're a beautiful, strong, and accomplished person and you need someone who *compliments* all those traits about you, not someone who completes you. When you're dating, know your worth and don't be afraid to walk away from that which does not serve you.

Don't Write Them Off Just Yet...

Have you ever been hit on by someone you felt wasn't exactly in your weight class? Maybe the barista at the café you like to go to for brunch or maybe the unreasonably gorgeous physical trainer at the gym. Maybe it's the professor who teaches at the university you volunteer at, who always takes the time out to talk to you but couldn't possibly be interested in you romantically.

As black women, we've been told from almost from our very beginnings that we're not nearly as desirable as our white counterparts. In 2016, a Google search for "beautiful women" was discovered to have revealed to be lacking any women of color (Tongco 2016). (This revelation by the public eventually caused Google to change its search features to include women of color). The interesting thing about that is just that in all likelihood, the search feature probably went unnoticed for years before several influencers happened to point it out and post it on their social media accounts. The reason why it went unnoticed is that whiteness in America is considered the norm. And in the way of how we, as black women, are viewed in this society, it's considered an uncommon thing for people, on the whole, to consider us as the standard of beauty.

But then, if you're as old as I am, this isn't news to you. When we were little girls and we saw Disney Princesses and superheroes and wanted to be like them, we also came to the realization that since none of them looked like us, there was no place for us there. In the nineties, in particular, television shows and movies, romances played out among white men and women smashed box office records while black stories went straight to video.

That idea is changing thanks to more diversity in our media, but a lot of us are still a little brainwashed when it comes to who we think we are in this world. For example, I knew a woman in her sixties who only dated men her age, even though men of *all* ages shot their shots almost every time we went out. One time, when we were out at brunch, a handsome man in his forties approached her and put on his strongest GQ game. Tragically, she just didn't see that he was flirting. The entire experience usually went right over her head, and he was sent back to his table with his proverbial tail between his legs.

We pass up opportunities because we can't fathom the idea that someone too different might actually be interested in us. We may also fear societal judgment. I'm here to tell you that if the connection is right, there's no reason not to explore the possibilities.

- **Young in Body does not equal Young in Mind.** Just like you don't feel like you're fifty, there are people who don't feel their age either. My opinion about dating younger is pretty straightforward. I think it's fine within reason (let me stress, *within reason*), and I don't think it should be a firm deal breaker. If the connection is there and every other piece fits (and obviously, the person is of legal age), then why should you count them out? I'm not saying you should pretend you're a thirty-year-old in order to date a thirty-year-old. What I mean is that if that person meets you where you're at and *compliments* your life, why would you reject him because of his age?

- **The manager at the Shake Shack is a viable option.** Okay, stay with me here. I know a lot of us want the ones with the good jobs, and I am all for that. But think for a second about why that is. Societally speaking, we look down our noses at certain jobs because that's what we've always been taught. Within the black community, there is the idea that, as a black woman, we need someone to take care of us financially. And don't get me wrong. It's a nice idea until you consider women like Oprah. Oprah Winfrey has more money than almost every woman in America, and if she wasn't with Stedman, just about *every* man she dated would be the equivalent of you dating the shoe salesman at Footlocker. In fact, as I understand it, Stedman is an accomplished man in his own right and probably still that exact equivalent. My point is that it's not the job title that you should be concerned about, but rather whether or not he is responsible and can take care of himself. At the end of the day, I feel it's more important that he's financially responsible and self-sufficient.

- **Interracial Dating.** I know there's a lot of debate about dating outside of your race, and personally, I've always been a different strokes for different folks kind of person. Since we all come from the older generation, we've all got our own ideas about the subject, and all I will say is the same as I have been saying: *If the connection is there, why fight it?* Now, being with someone outside of your own race will bring some challenges, and for that, I completely understand some of you who don't want to go down that road. The point I want to make is that if the person is right for you, you'll realize you won't be alone in those challenges. If they align with your values and beliefs, and most importantly, celebrate your differences (as opposed to ignoring them. Don't fall into the "I don't see color" trap), then I say go for it. You might learn something you didn't know about their culture, just as they will learn something about yours.

- **The beautiful people.** Ever meet somebody who just looks unreal? Like, have you ever met a man who actually looked like Jason Momoa? It's completely unbelievable in broad daylight, right? Now imagine that Jason Momoa is into you. Can't even wrap your mind around it, can you? People like that don't just go for ordinary women, right? Wrong. You're a catch! Of course, beautiful people want to get to know you too, and why shouldn't they? Didn't you know you were beautiful too? Don't be afraid to date above your pay grade!

The Second Chance

After almost forty years of marriage, Jillian lost her husband in 2019 to COVID. He was her first and only love, as they met when they were fifteen and sixteen. As high school sweethearts, they dated exclusively all through school, and when it was time to go to college, they applied and got into the same university.

Throughout their lives, they were inseparable for much of their lives. They worked in the same field of study, and while they didn't always work for the same companies, they always seemed to be aligned in work as well as their personal life. They were the epitome of a perfect couple.

You can imagine how heartbreaking it was for Jillian to lose him after four decades of love and marriage. Practically speaking, when he died, he'd left her with enough money to live comfortably, plus her family all chipped in to help her where they could. But emotionally, it was the hardest time of Jillian's life. She couldn't imagine having to live in a world where her husband wasn't a part of it.

After a few months of mourning, her friend suggested she seek out a support group for widows to help her feel like she wasn't alone. Feeling like she had nothing to lose, Jillian decided to give it a try, hoping to connect with people who had gone through or were going through a similar experience.

In those weekly meetings, she started connecting with people of all ages and from all walks of life. Men and women who'd all been through what she had gone through and many of them suffering the same type of loss due to the devastating effect the pandemic had on our country.

Over time, she began feeling better about herself and even started considering dating again. However, Jillian was nearly sixty years old, and she felt embarrassed at the idea of being with someone else when the only relationship she'd ever had was gone. What would her children think? What would her church family and friends think??

Among the friends that she'd started to make, Jillian befriended a fellow member of the support group, Steve. He was about ten years her junior and he worked at the local automotive plant. He was entirely different from Jillian's late husband in many ways. He was shorter than him and worked with his hands even outside of work. But he was kind and smart and very handsome and he always had a cup of coffee ready for her when she came to the support group meetings. He originally came from the

STRIDE

South and still had a lot of family there and even carried a lot of old-school gentleman habits and mentalities.

As they grew closer, Steve asked her out to a movie. Completely blindsided, Jillian rejected him, even though she kind of wanted to go. It had been so long since she enjoyed a night out with anyone. And going out with Steve, who she got along with fabulously, sounded like her kind of night.

Steve would ask her out twice more over the next month, and each time, she'd tell him no. Until one evening after the group meeting, he'd ask her if she wasn't ready to date yet.

"No," she told him, "It's not that. It's just...well, what would people say?"

Steve, being the smart aleck kind of man, answered, "I guess they'll say good for us for living."

Jillian gave his words a lot of thought. She started questioning whether she was truly living her life to the fullest. She realized that she hadn't been. Her late husband would have wanted her to be happy, and the more she thought about it, the more she realized that Steve made her happier than she'd been since her husband's passing.

The next day, she called him up and asked him out. He accepted, of course. They got married last year in a private ceremony.

CHAPTER SIX

Love and Marriage

"Black Love is about building a life
that's filled with adventure, passion,
and purpose."

— Issa Rae

Sitting on the Dock of the Bay

I've been looking forward to retirement for about as long as I've been working. I remember my first job at sixteen and thinking about how if I just saved up all my money, I could retire early at thirty and live the life, lying out on the beach and soaking up the sun. Working when you're young can be tough, especially when you haven't found your true calling yet.

But now we're either retired or approaching retirement age. And if we're married, then we might find ourselves looking across the dinner table in our empty nest, wondering what comes next.

You'd be interested to know that American adults between the ages of 65 and 74 have a divorce rate of about 43 percent, the highest among divorce rates. And among black couples that number jumps to 49 percent (Butrica and Smith 2012). Why, you might ask? Well, I could give you a laundry list of reasons, according to researchers who have been studying married couples for decades, but if you're looking at your spouse right now and you can't stand the way they chew, then you already know the answer.

When you're married, you share your life and everything that comes with it. Your attention, oftentimes, is divided between children, work, and whatever else life throws at you. Married life at thirty feels more like it's you and your love against the world.

Whereas married life at fifty and over...well...not so much. The drama has probably died down. The kids have moved out. You get up in the morning and have your cup of coffee, and suddenly you notice that your mate smacks when they eat cornflakes or the sound of their fork when it scrapes the plate just grates your nerves. In the land of retirement, it's just you and your spouse on an island. And it doesn't matter if you travel or take ballroom classes together, it's still just you and them, staring at each other across the dining room table.

I know. It sounds bleak. But it doesn't have to be. Marriage is a lifelong commitment between beings that shift and change in body and mind (and sometimes in spirit). The challenge when you retire is getting to know each other as mature people with lives very different from the one you entered into initially. If you're feeling some type of way with your spouse now that you're older, all is not lost. You just need to recalibrate, readjust, and get into a new groove.

You Don't Have to Do Everything Together

I feel like this is something that we should know by now. When you've been married a certain number of years, you figure out that while it's nice to do things together, every now and then you or your spouse might feel like there might be a thing or two that you can do apart. It's usually not a big deal in a healthy marriage. You might want a night out with the girls, and he might want a night out with the guys and it's fine.

It doesn't feel like a big deal until you're retired and can't seem to get away from one another. Or sometimes it's the opposite. Maybe your partner has been going to the gym every week since you've been together, and suddenly, you can't understand why you shouldn't go together. Whatever the case, it's entirely normal to look up and realize that you want some change in your personal dynamic.

But the trick is recognizing it and planning together what works for you. Here are some suggestions of activities you can do together or separately.

- **Together Activities:**

  » **Dance classes.** Funny how we keep coming back to dance. If your partner likes to cut a rug every now and then, maybe take some classes together. Preferably something where you have to hold each other like salsa or ballroom. Physical touch can help keep your connection strong.

  » **Game nights.** The game isn't important but consider things that you have to work together to play. Cards and board games are good, but if you're feeling adventurous and want to try something different, consider an Escape Room. These rooms require teamwork and putting your heads together to solve a mystery. While most rooms can accommodate up to 12 people, you can solve one as a duo just as easily.

» **Couples spa/massage.** Couples massages or spa nights are a great way to reconnect with your loved one through relaxation together. You might think that sitting around on a couch and watching television can be defined as relaxing together, but experiencing a massage together on a table can take you to a whole new level of relaxation. It's a chance to reach a higher state of relaxation with your partner that you may not have considered before.

» **Taking on a project together.** Building or creating something together is a great way to keep comradery between you, but keep in mind that whatever project you choose *you both need to be on board*. You deciding to rebuild a car with your husband when you have no interest in doing so is only going to result in anger and resentment should one of you lose interest. Choose something you both will enjoy.

- **Not Together Activities:**

  - » **Weekly/monthly movie night.** Sure, you could do this one together, but when you watch a movie together, you're normally not communicating or connecting in any way and when looking for activities to bring you together, movies aren't as good at that unless you plan on holding entire conversations during the movie (which would probably get you tossed out of the theatre if you do it too much). Plus, let's say your mate is into Marvel movies and that's just not your jam. Why not go out to see what you want by yourself? It's only a couple of hours and when you come back, you might have the chance to tell your spouse all about it (Hint: That's a great way to pique your spouse's interest and make them enjoy the same movies eventually).

  - » **Doing your own project.** Unlike the last section where we discussed doing a project together, this one focuses on doing the one thing you've always wanted to take on. Now is the time to write that novel or build a birdhouse or even rebuild a car of your own. The goal is to make time to do something that requires only your attention and gives you a little space. Mentally speaking, doing a project on your own can give you a little bit of a bandwidth break from social activities and such.

» **Start a book club.** Yes, you could join one too, but have you ever considered starting one with your friends? I never did before the pandemic. When the libraries closed in my neighborhood, a few girlfriends and I decided to start a book club with a focus on women authors of color. It was an enlightening and fun time once a month that was just for me. When I got home to my husband, it was like a reset. Being in a room with my peers for a few hours brought me back to reality.

» **Day trips.** I know there are a lot of women out there who are reluctant to go on a trip without their spouse. But we're not talking about going to Jamaica for a week. Instead, consider taking a day trip. Depending on where you live, there are cabins, spas, and resorts in your area where you can go and spend a quiet day just being with yourself. I wouldn't recommend doing this weekly (or even monthly) but taking the time to do it occasionally can be beneficial for your well-being.

Gramma and Paw-Paw!

Being a grandparent can be an exciting experience. When my oldest child had my first grandson, I was elated. The idea of little feet pitter-pattering around my house filled me with such joy that I momentarily forgot that he wasn't *my* child. I don't know what happens to your brain when you become a grandparent, but something inside you starts to bond with the new life even before they're born and you start thinking of them as yours.

That's not a bad thing, really. It makes it easier when they come to visit or if they should end up living with you because of life changes. Having a relationship with the new little person in your life is the natural order of things so you should indulge in your new role as grandmother.

Ideally, your role as a grandparent isn't a parental role, but I think within our community oftentimes it can become one. When something goes wrong, your children might end up leaning on you to help them raise their children. It's a dynamic that exists because of centuries of abuse and displacement of our ancestors. Sticking together as a family has been encoded in our blood.

That being said, these days, this next generation is hard at work at healing our generational trauma and our roles as grandparents are turning into...well, grandparents. You know, just like we used to see in the movies, a lot of us visit our grandbabies every once in a while instead of all of us living under the same roof. And I'm not criticizing it. I'm just saying that your role as grandmother might not be the same as the one that your mother had. Here are a few things to keep in mind.

- **You do not have to raise these kids (probably).** Keep in mind that I'm not referring to grandparents in special situations who have to raise their grandchildren. For those of us whose children have waited to have their own children or are in better situations than we were, we should not assume that they need our help in teaching their kids to read. They've got that on lock, and we need to recognize that's the case and fast. I know it was hard because I know plenty of grandmothers in my generation who practically raised my friends while their parents were in college or at work all day. Most of us only have experiences pulled from grandmothers with regular input in their lives. Today's grandmothers are not necessarily that. Don't take that too hard, though. You get to spoil your grandchildren in ways that you may never have experienced with your own children.

- **Respect your children's wishes**. I know this one is a hard one for a lot of us. We were raised to take our parent's word as gospel. What they said went even after we were grown, *and* whatever they wanted to do with our children, we had to go along with it. If you're on that train, I hate to be the one to tell you that is not how grandparenting works anymore. Your children are much healthier people than the ones who raised us and they know that as adults, they have the right to raise their children however they want...and you have to respect that. You might not like that your grandson's hair is too long, but if mom and dad want it that way, you *have to respect it*. Don't get yourself shut out just because you think it's your way or the highway.

- **You now have McDonald's money!** Speaking of spoiling your kids, look forward to treating them to things you might not have been able to with your own children. As an empty nester, you may find that you have more disposable income and that means that when you're out with your grandbabies, you can say yes way more often than you ever could. A warning, though: your own children might get a little jealous.

Changes

Arlene had an average childhood for a black family in the '70s. Her mother was widowed at a young age and had to raise her and her sister on her own. Having very little money, Arlene's mother often left her and her sister with their grandmother while she went to work during the day. Sometimes they would be there for eight hours, and when their mother had to work double shifts, they would stay overnight.

This resulted in their grandmother being the primary guardian over them most days, which wasn't a bad thing. Their grandmother took them to church every day and had them both baptized when they were old enough. She read to them every day from when they were small, giving them a head start in school. Every bump and bruise she nursed, and when they were old enough to start dating, she was usually the one the girls went to for advice in dating.

Arlene's mother was there as well and did what she could do, but as a working mother, much of her input into their lives was limited. Despite doing her best as most black mothers do, it wasn't easy. She was thankful to have her grandmother there to be for her and her sister.

Time passed and Arlene grew up and married a man she met in college. They had four children and lived in the suburbs of Chicago. Arlene worked as a chemical engineer, and her husband was an attorney. They were able to have a good life and make a better life than she was raised in.

When Arlene became a grandmother, she relied on her own upbringing and became overly involved in her children's lives when it came to her grandbabies. She came over to her children's houses unannounced all the time. When the grandchildren were in her care, she ignored everything her children asked her to do and treated her grandchildren as though they were her own in every overbearing way possible.

It all came to a head one day when she decided to take her youngest granddaughter to get her hair cut *without telling her son.* When her son found out, he exploded and vowed never to bring the child back unless she learned to respect his and his wife's wishes. Confused, Arlene couldn't understand what she'd done wrong. After all, wasn't it her job to raise these children as she would her own?

The answer? No. It wasn't. As a grandparent, she had to learn the hard way to defer to her son's wishes for their child's wellbeing. It would take the better part of a year for her to get back into her son's good graces, but once she had, she promised never to make major decisions about her grandchildren without consulting her son first. Arlene learned that being a grandparent today is way different than it's ever been. Fortunately for her, she didn't have to lose her grandchildren to figure that out.

PART THREE

Growth and Purpose

CHAPTER SEVEN

Learning How to Live

> "Be Present in all things and thankful
> for all things."
> — Maya Angelou

Rebranding the "Bucket List"

I've never been a big fan of the term "Bucket List" because, for me, it just puts a negative light on the whole idea of living for today. In fact, it just never sounded like living for today to me at all. More like "Rushing to get it all done before you die." Here's a fun fact. The term "Bucket List" is defined Merriam Webster as "a list of things that one has not done before but wants to do before dying" (Merriam Webster n.d.) and has only been in a part of our pop culture vernacular since 2007 when the movie *The Bucket List* came out.

If you haven't seen the film, it stars Jack Nicholson as an elderly billionaire who meets up with a mechanic played by Morgan Freeman in a hospital, and they discover they have something in common. There are a ton of things they've never done that they'd like to do before they kick the proverbial bucket. Hence, they make a, you guessed it, bucket list.

Now, I don't disagree with the concept entirely. As black women of a certain age, we've been conditioned to believe that we're only supposed to participate in certain activities. Many of the things we may have wanted to try are largely decried as being outside of our culture or White People Stuff (WPS), colloquially speaking, and thus not for us to participate in.

While I will say there are certain activities that I believe people of color shouldn't do for the sake of safety, I think completely closing yourself off to the majority of life experiences just closes your world entirely. And while we've been told to stay away from many things, we were told more for the sake of keeping ourselves safe. Many of us go our entire lives without gaining very many wonderful life experiences.

So, let's start with a rebrand of the "Bucket List" label. Instead of focusing on things we *should* do before we die, let's focus on what we *can* do to make our worlds bigger and nourish our lives right now.

The Moment

That sounds much better, doesn't it? Maybe it's my flair for the dramatic, but I prefer to call this practice creating "moments" instead of making a bucket list. Every religious and spiritual practice alludes to being in the moment as much as possible in your life. I know you've heard the term "Tomorrow isn't promised" or maybe "Be Here Now." Even the scientific study of time reminds us that we only have the moment we're living in. The second it took you to read that last sentence is already gone. And so's that one. And this one too. You are alive and kicking right this second. The next second doesn't exist until you've experienced it.

Since we are alive right now in this very second, think about *what* you want to do or *where* you want to be. The next second is just around the corner and the next and the next. Where do you want that path of seconds to lead you? And most importantly, do you want to get to that moment where your life has shifted into something you could never have imagined?

Let's explore some possible *moments* that you could be experiencing.

- **Angels in the Architecture**. So, you want to travel. You probably always wanted to go to France, Italy, or Jamaica and sit out in the sun. But have you considered traveling to Egypt to see the Pyramids? Or walking through Merdeka Square in Jakarta? Maybe going on safari in the African Savanna. There's a distinct difference between seeing the world and going on vacation. Whilst I'm not knocking down going on vacation, imagine traveling out of the country (or even out of state) and coming home with a new point of view. This world is so much bigger than your backyard, so why not explore it?

- **Yes, you can eat that.** I have a friend whose mother has never tasted cheesecake of any kind because she could never grasp the concept of cheese being a dessert. I wish I was joking about that. But she's like that with a lot of food. Anything that she doesn't recognize or might seem foreign, she rejects without even tasting it and has lived her whole life this way. I'm sure more than a few of you can relate. Something too far out of our comfort zone is hard for us to try. But I'll tell you from experience that the best food I've ever had has been food I never would have thought to enjoy. So, the next time you go out to eat (or maybe on your next trip to another country), try something completely new. You'll be surprised how many great foods are out there to enjoy.

- **Connect with another culture.** There are a few ways to go about this. If you've decided to learn another language, take the extra step and learn something about the culture that the language comes from. Not only will it help you learn the language faster, but it'll also give you context for the structure of the language and you might actually end up seeing the beauty in it. Or try getting to know someone outside of your own culture. You might think you know a lot about the Middle Eastern or Latin family that lives in your neighborhood, but you probably know a lot less than you think. And when you get to know them, you'll not only find commonalities, but you'll learn about customs and traditions that you never experienced before.

- **Go hiking/camping regularly.** This is one that I've seen discussed heavily as WPS, and personally, I can see why. Media has taught us that white folks get killed or lost in the woods, so why on earth would we ever go there? First of all, there's nothing wrong with connecting with nature. With a little preparation (I'd highly advise going with someone more knowledgeable than you), you'll find that the great outdoors is a wonder that's just outside your back door.

Skydiving Grandma

When I think of being adventurous, the first thing that comes to mind is an old cartoon my kids watched when they were young. The cartoon was called *Hoodwinked* and it was a reimagining of the *Little Red Riding Hood* story. In the movie, Little Red Riding Hood's grandmother was secretly an extreme sports junkie who jumped out of airplanes and snowboarded in the X Games.

Okay, I'm not trying to encourage you to go skydiving, unless that happens to be one of your moments and you're in good health. In which case, I'd say go for it (more on that later), but you can step a little out of your comfort zone when it comes to living your life. Being adventurous doesn't have to be a literal translation, after all. All it means is taking a little bit of risk in your life. For example:

- **Reading is fundamental**. Ever pick up a book that you never thought you'd read? Or read something on the recommendation of someone else? Admittedly, it can be hit or miss, but you shouldn't let that deter you. Reading something new can expose you to things you didn't know existed. Lives that you never knew could be lived. Dive into a genre you've avoided before or an author you never even thought to read. A long time ago, I adopted the philosophy of not focusing on a book's genre when selecting what to read. In doing that, I've read books that were beautiful in their scope of prose as well as clunky and ham-fisted in their delivery. I've laughed harder than I've ever laughed in my life, and I've discovered new ways a story can be told. Personally, as a writer, reading a variety of books has made me better. It's also made me step into others' shoes to understand better the lives of those that aren't mine.

- **Go skydiving.** I know I just said don't. Actually, I said don't if your health precludes it. But I don't just mean skydiving. If you're healthy enough to try it, get into some sports that get your heart racing. Cross-country skiing, surfing or boogie boarding, roller skating, etc. Fun high-octane sports activities can give you a good reason to stay in shape and have the experience of a lifetime.

- **Fear is a great motivator**. This one is tough to overcome, but in keeping with the last tip, consider doing the one thing that you're terrified of doing. Conquering a fear can be extremely therapeutic (Hull 2020). And fears can come in many forms. From a fear of heights to a fear of lima beans, taking on something that terrifies you and conquering it can give you a shot of confidence that you didn't know was underneath.

Seeing the Trees

Taking hold of the moments and running with them can shift everything in your life, and, believe it or not, it can bring you peace in a way that you never considered. So much of our lives is spent worrying about what will happen tomorrow or fretting over the details of that event we're hosting or that trip we're going on in three months that we usually end up letting the rest of our lives pass us by.

You've heard that old saying "not seeing the forest for the trees" as an indictment of not seeing the big picture. Not taking hold of your moments is a lot like doing that in reverse. If you don't take in the beauty of the trees, how can you know that the forest is beautiful? If you're sitting down and reading this, take a moment to examine your surroundings. Listen to the breath that you're taking in or the clock ticking on the wall. If you're barefoot, feel the softness of the carpet under you. These are things that you don't tend to notice because you're already in the future or the past. What does your life feel like right now?

- **Take joy in the little things.** We all love it when the big stuff happens. My daughter's wedding, for example, was one of the great highlights of my life, as I'm sure events like that can be for most of you reading this. But what about the little things? The taste of a fresh strawberry or the feel of a cool breeze when you take a walk. One of the most precious times of my life was during a walk while listening to a classical music playlist. The sound of violins against the beautiful blue sky took me away from all my future worries and placed me right there on the wooded trail outside my home. Now, whenever I get a little stressed, I try to go back to that moment in my mind or try to find it while exercising. It's such a small thing, but it's brought me back to life more times than I can count.

- **Digital detoxes are important.** Disconnect from the internet for a while. In fact, disconnect from all your electronics every so often. Studies show that disconnecting from the internet can reduce your anxiety and increase your productivity (Martinez 2023). It can also help you with meaningful connections with others in your life. I can't tell you how much work I get done when I disconnect from the internet in one way or another. I have a computer in my home that has no access to the internet. It has no games on it, and it only has about 4MB of RAM. It is completely obsolete. And why? Because for a few hours a day, I need to be present in order to create. I need to feel the keyboard under my fingers and the silence of my room. I need to be here with you while I write these words. When you disconnect from the noise, you'll find that you move in a different way than before.

- **Be. Here. Now.** I can't express that enough in this chapter. Sometimes fear can hold us back or keep us from experiencing or expressing our best selves, something I've always found to be tragic for black women. The world has been telling us to dim our lights for so long that many of us have just automatically given up on doing anything that might make our lives more fulfilled. Just the act of being conscious of yourself right now can shift your focus to getting to know the person that you are. Feeling where you're right in this moment is essential for you to start down the path toward living your best possible life. So take a breath. Open your eyes. And be right here, right now. Enjoy this moment because it's the only one you have.

Belinda's Tattoo

Belinda was an artist. She enjoyed painting landscape pictures and loved art in general. If you talked to her about art, she'd go on and on about such things as composition and lighting and the brushstrokes of the greats. She loved working in watercolors and oils, in charcoal and chalk. She enjoyed the idea of creating something beautiful on a canvas.

And the one thing that Belinda has always wanted was a tattoo. Over the years, she'd given a million different reasons why she never got one. At first, she believed only a certain type of person got tattoos (or at least, that's what her mother always said). Then, when she got older, it became a fear of the pain involved. And when she turned fifty-five, she thought she was too old for tattoos.

One day, her daughter decided that she was going to get a tattoo of her own. Belinda, already having her own ideas about tattoos, objected to the entire thing. "You're a mother," was the first thing she pointed out. "What will your children think? And what are you going to do when you get old? Can you imagine being in a nursing home covered in tattoos??"

Belinda and her daughter debated it for months before her daughter finally decided what she would get. On the day of her appointment, she invited her mother along. At first, Belinda said no. There was no way she would watch her daughter be in pain just to mark up her body. Plus, it was permanent. *Permanent.* To Belinda, it was just another way to damage her skin.

"Mom," she told her, "I'm just beautifying my temple. It's no different than if you painted a mural."

"I still don't like it," she objected.

"Well, why don't you just come with me before you decide that you don't like it? You've never seen one before, so why not?"

Belinda reluctantly agreed and went with her daughter to her appointment. When they got to the tattoo shop,

Belinda looked at the tattoo artist skeptically. She judged his heavily tattooed arms and asked him what his family thought of them. To his credit, the tattoo artist took her judgment in stride and handled her jabs by answering her calmly and truthfully.

After a while, her daughter was in the chair and Belinda watched the process. She expected to see a horror show of blood and her daughter writhing in agony. Instead, she saw her daughter relaxed on a reclining chair while the tattoo artist traced a beautifully drawn heart on her daughter's wrist. She watched the artist open up individual packs of ink and needles, exhibiting as much hygiene as possible.

And then, when the tattooing began, Belinda found that she was fascinated by the way he was able to create a beautiful picture with the aid of vibrating needles. When it was done, it was so stunningly beautiful to Belinda that she felt a little bad for giving him a hard time.

She walked out with her daughter, marveling at the tattoo. Her daughter asked her, "See, that wasn't so bad was it?"

"No...I guess it wasn't. I just thought that it would be so much worse than it was."

"So did I," she said, "But I figured I should get over my fear at some point. Right?"

Belinda thought about that. And about how fear had run her entire experience surrounding the subject. That evening, she decided to research tattoos as an art form and discovered there were ancient cultures that attributed their lifestyle around the telling of stories through tattoos. Even African cultures engaged in tattoos and scarification (which she'd always thought was something that only "white people" did.)

She still wasn't too keen on the pain, but now she wanted the experience of having beautiful tattoos on her skin. She began by trying out henna tattoos, which were semi-permanent. Initially, she learned from someone else, but later, she taught herself. Eventually, Belinda decided the day had come when she'd get her own real tattoo.

And she did a few years later. A heart on the opposite wrist as her daughter.

CHAPTER EIGHT

Money Matters

"I deserve to be prosperous."
— Patrice Washington

For the Love of Money

I think that the money discussion varies among black women around our age. If I'm talking to women older than fifty, then that means I'm addressing those of us who belong to the Gen X generation and beyond. I'd like to think that we all got some education on how to manage our money, particularly those of us who are Gen Xers and have witnessed our mothers struggle during times of divorce or being widowed.

You see, many of us didn't get a proper education into how to handle our money for the long run. Oh, we may have gotten the *get a good job and be independent* speeches in the later generations, but that was usually coupled with the mixed message that we need to find a good man with a good job who will support us. I know that doesn't make any sense. I've often found myself wondering what exactly does the world want from us?

Have you ever heard one of those intensely misogynistic podcasts where men describe their ideal women as being independent with a good job and her own money but also looking for a man with a good job and his own money so that he can support her? And then, if she actually uses her own money or earns more money than him, she's considered "too independent" and therefore of low value? Confusing, isn't it?

It's no wonder so many of us don't know which way to jump when it comes to money. And while the wage gap between black women and white men is still at 63 cents per dollar, according to the Government Accountability Office, black women are still behind everyone else in terms of the wage divide. That is to say, even white women (who are disproportionately making less than white men) are making more than we are. Now, we can blame a lot of that on sexism and racism, but I'm inclined to think that women our age still don't have the whole money thing locked down for a lot of other reasons. Sure, some of us have had the presence of mind to sock away some money in a separate bank account that perhaps your spouse doesn't know about, but honestly, you shouldn't even have to do that. Your money and the management of it is important and we shouldn't be ashamed of that.

It's Never Too Late

Part of the reason black women over fifty are still not financially secure is that many of us have given up on saving our money. You start to think that you're fifty and therefore there won't be enough time to save up for retirement. I suppose if you're thinking conventionally, that might be true. Putting away part of your paycheck that you use to buy coffee in the mornings won't really get you to where you need to be in fifteen years.

It's all about thinking of better ways to manage your money and living frugally now to avoid stress when you're older. Here are a few things to think about:

- **You may have to work well past your retirement.** I hate to be the one to say it, but that's the reality you might be facing. We all look forward to retirement after years and years of working, but the hard reality is that the retirement funds you get from the government may not be enough just yet. But that's not necessarily a bad thing. A lot of women I know purposely chose to stay working so they can have a chance to save as well as build up their retirement fund through the government. If that turns out to be the case for you, don't stress about it. It might turn out to be a bigger check for you later.

- **There's no such thing as getting rich fast.** This is how a lot of us fall into scams that target older women specifically. When the average life span for a black woman is 74 years old (Arias 2022), a lot of us resort to get-rich-quick schemes for a big payout. I'm here to tell you that it just doesn't exist outside of the off chance that you might win the lottery. A rule of thumb I always keep is that if it sounds too good to be true, it is. Don't give that Nigerian Prince your money or let anyone con you into logging onto your computer to steal money from your bank account. If it looks like an easy way to get money, don't you fall for it. I promise you it's not.

- **It's okay if you don't have millions.** I think that my generation, in particular, has the idea in our minds that by this age, we're supposed to be sitting on a pile of money. If you're not, don't feel like you've failed. There are a lot of factors that go into black women and whether or not we have any money at all by the time we're over fifty. As I mentioned before, the racial disparity and wage divide in America has had its boot on our neck for a very long time. Not to mention the rate of inflation in this country has made it so that many people are having a harder time than ever at making a livable wage. Chances are high that you had to work hard for every dime you got and that should be commended. You've been working against insurmountable odds, and for that, you've done an exceptional job.

Maybe It's Not the Coffee

Do you remember when people used to say that if you cut out frivolous things like a morning coffee in the morning, you could save an insane amount of money in no time?

I remember in my youth hearing someone say to me, "If you have a Starbucks coffee every morning and you just cut that out, you could save 300,000 dollars by the end of the year!" Yeah, I don't know what math people were using back then, but I think an entire generation of us got it in our minds that little cuts are all that we need to get our money right. The thing is, they're about half right. Little cuts do help. Cooking dinner at home instead of eating out or scaling back on luxury expenses does make a difference, but if you think that you'll have enough money to retire early, think again.

It's true that cutting out Starbucks coffee is a good idea if you want to improve your spending habits. As black women, we have been taught by society and culture to be strong, independent, and have our own money and be the "boss" or a "baddie" or however they're putting it these days. We got all these messages without any usable strategies as to how to do that. So, here we are. Over fifty and looking down the road at retirement.

I don't have all the answers, but I can give you a few tips that helped me along the way.

- **Spread it around.** When it comes to things like joint bank accounts and savings plans, it's natural to want to combine them for the good of the entire household. Seems like common sense, doesn't it? It may come at a surprise that more than fifty percent of all divorces are due to financial issues within the marriage (Lee, et al. 2021). If you've ever had an argument over who spent what out of the joint bank account, you can understand why. The bottom line is that if you were ever told to sock away "rainy day" money outside of a joint bank account, that's actually not bad advice. I would take it a step further and consider not getting a joint account in the first place. Practically speaking, it's harder to save when someone else also has a hand in your pocket. Get separate accounts.

- **Financial advisors are for everyone**. Did you know you could have a financial advisor without making 100,000 dollars a year? It's true. Most people are under the impression that only the rich ever consulted one, but here's a fun fact. Financial Advisors are not just for rich people. The job of a financial advisor is to make a workable budget for you to not only live off of but to save off of as well. They can also advise you on appropriate investments and savings plans that work for your situation.

- **Don't even bother with a savings account**. Listen, I'm not saying you shouldn't, but rather, you should have a better understanding of what savings accounts are good for, especially at this stage in our lives. The truth is that a savings account is only beneficial if you have a large amount of money that you want to sit on for a while. Or perhaps to have as a fallback if you need money for a car repair or to replace a major appliance. We tend to think of savings accounts as a way to make our money grow when we should be thinking of it more like a piggy bank. If you're looking at ways to grow your money, consider CDs or IRAs instead. These savings plans have the sole purpose of building up your money through investments and/or interest rates so that you end up with more than what you put in.

- **Finessing your budget**. Yeah, you could go entirely minimalist and cut out every luxury you have to save money. But we're talking a lot about the *quality* of your life as well as *quantity* in this book. Listen, I don't want to pay for streaming services, but I also want to watch my Netflix when I want to relax. So instead of cutting it, I budget for it. Similarly, for things I use less often, I find inexpensive options. For instance, I used to have bookshelves of untouched books in my house. Then, one day, I thought about the fact that I love to read, but I generally only read a book once. I don't even reference it again, usually thanks to the internet. So, consider activities and items similar to that and look for other alternatives. Instead of buying books, go to the library and check them out. Instead of eating out for dinner, consider signing up for a food service program where you cook at home. I did this and discovered the money I paid for the service evened out to groceries I might have bought *and* kept me from spending too much on takeout. You might end up learning or improving a new skill as well as saving money just by finessing your budget a little.

Investing Isn't for All of Us

Okay, so let's say for the sake of argument that you've gotten lucky and fallen into a nice chunk of money. Maybe you've sold your house or a relative left you some money. However it happened, you've got a bunch of money burning a hole in your pocket. So, what do you do with it?

Most people would tell you to invest your money. And it's sound advice, but— can we talk about that for real, though? What exactly do you know about investing your money? I'm willing to bet that unless you're in the investment banking business or have personally educated yourself on it for years, you probably don't know a whole lot.

Let's get something straight. Investment is a great thing to do with your money. A really great thing, in fact. The right investments can ensure you never have to worry about money for the rest of your life. But the wrong investments can put you in the poorhouse. Having no real knowledge of investing can lead you to lose everything in a heartbeat.

If you're going to invest your money, it is in your best interest to know as much about it as possible. That being said:

- **Get a basic education**. Over the past few years, there has been an influx of investment apps that not only allow you to invest in small amounts (or big if you're so inclined) but offer articles and educational tips about investing. Companies like Acorns and Stash pride themselves on making investing easy for everyone. With some apps, you have the option to invest in packages that align with what you want to support. Like if you're into the environment, there are packages with companies that specialize in just that. While other aps will take small amounts of money out of every purchase you make and put it toward your selected investment. Through these companies, you'll have the opportunity to get an education so that you can make better choices in your investments.

- **Become financially literate**. While I don't expect everyone to become an expert overnight, it absolutely cannot hurt to adopt financial literacy as your special interest. Look for classes or programs at your local library. If they don't have any, suggest them to the librarian. On your own, look into some books that can help you get started, like Adam Rose's 9 *Money Habits Keeping You Poor* or Paris Woods' *The Black Girl's Guide to Financial Freedom*. Both books break down the subject in terms you can work with without using difficult to understand jargon.

- **Remember when I told you about a Financial Advisor?** Yeah, that applies here, not just with figuring out your budget and savings but also with investing. Listen, if you're just not interested in learning how to invest, don't sweat it. Most people just want to live their lives and not think about the details. The great thing about an advisor is that their scope isn't just through your immediate needs. Anything financially speaking, they can help you with *and* help you avoid any future pitfalls.

- **Investing isn't just stocks.** Literally speaking, all investing your money is putting your money into something that will net you a profit. Yes, that includes stocks, but it also includes housing, owning land, or small businesses. When you start to think of it this way, you'll start to think of building a legacy as well as creating an income source. For example, if you buy land, you can use it to build a home for your family or for someone to rent out and create passive income. The only caveat to this is be careful. The bad investment rule applies here. Know everything about where you're putting your money beforehand.

Plan B

Beatrice was married to her husband for forty years until he left her. On the day of their divorce, she discovered that her husband used the money in their joint savings account for gambling and lost almost everything that they'd saved up over their years together.

Now, Beatrice was no fool. She knew that her husband had a gambling problem and a great number of other issues as well. And while they were married, Beatrice did whatever she had to in order to keep them both afloat. She often worked two jobs just to keep food on the table.

Fifteen years ago, her husband won a large amount of money, and they lost it all in a matter of hours the next day. Right then, she almost left him. Distraught over his reckless behavior, she left for a while to stay at her sister's house. While there, she cried over her husband. Heartbroken that he might be so careless.

"Leave him," her sister said at first. "He's not worth it." They argued over that for a while; however, Beatrice was determined to stand by her man. She'd been raised to weather the storm with her husband and she was determined to do so. After the third day of Beatrice's stay, her sister told her advice that would come to protect her for years later on.

"If you're not going to leave him, then get yourself a separate bank account."

At first, Beatrice brushed her sister off. Getting a separate bank account just sounded like stabbing her husband in the back. They were in this together, after all. But the more she thought about it, the more she realized how much she'd had to endure because their money was always tied up in his debts. She decided to take her sister's advice.

She stayed with her husband for the remaining twenty-five years until he finally wiped out their joint bank account. However, by that time, Beatrice had not only a separate account but several other investments and savings plans. When he filed for divorce from her, Beatrice had enough money to get a good attorney and ended up coming out on top in the end. Her husband, having squandered his relationship and their money, ended up with nothing, while Beatrice lives well to this day. All because she had a Plan B.

CHAPTER NINE

Your Legacy

"I've learned in life that what you give to others is what provides the most value to your life. There I was, a mess myself, yet I still had something to offer that would have an effect on another person's world."

— Jenifer Lewis, The Mother of Black Hollywood

What We Leave Behind

In his last comedy special on Netflix, comedian Deon Cole described this time of our lives as a measurement of summers. In talking about being on the set of *Blackish* with actress and comedian Jenifer Lewis, he comments how they played around with each other on set (as friends will do), and one day Lewis said to him, "You will not disrespect me nor my fifteen summers!" (Cole 2019).

His segment on the idea that once you pass forty, you've only got about thirty summers left hit a lot of us that saw it pretty hard. Well, it hit me pretty hard. The thing is, I don't think that any of us realistically believe that we will live forever, but I think it's something that, just as human beings, we don't think about or even like to think about. And I think it's because we're worried about what we will have to leave behind for the next generations.

For many black families, legacy is a big deal. How many cookouts or family reunions have you been to where you were treated to long and rambling stories about your great-auntie and her ten children? Or introduced to half a dozen cousins or uncles that you haven't seen since you were an infant? All of that, which we might've thought was just noise, has now become our role in the black family. You're the holder of a piece of the black family's legacy whether you like it or not. And that's a good thing. You have a new degree of respect in your family and in your community. We are elders now and we're revered as such.

Sounds really good when I put it like that, doesn't it? I hope so because this is a good thing. Now is the time for us to reflect on the legacy we're leaving for our communities. Although our approach may differ from that of our mothers and grandmothers, the key lies in how you go about it. And in keeping with the theme of this book, our generation gets the chance to do it in a way that not only enhances the lives of others around us but also uplifts us.

The Great Legacy

Family is important to us as black women, and so is knowing our history. Unfortunately, I don't have to tell many of you that it can be difficult to trace our family lineup to a certain point. Modern apps and programs like Ancestry have made it a little easier to find our relatives, but it can still be a struggle. In most of our families, that task usually falls on one or two people to know the family tree, but even if we do, there's still a lot of information that we just don't know or don't get.

I don't think I have to say why. Most of us know that at a certain point, many birth records were lost or obscured due to slavery, war, and other travesties done to the black population in America. While we may not have access to all the information we need, we should preserve whatever we do have. And in the vein of preserving your legacy, you can also honor your ancestors at the same time.

The thing is, we live in a time where some would like to erase our history altogether. There are people outside of the black community who would love nothing more than for everything that brought us to where we are today to be completely erased from history. There are laws being passed in the southern states as I write this that aim to miseducate the next generation and, well, I'm just going to tell it like it is. We simply can't let that happen.

In studying your own family history, you are, in your own small way, preserving the history of this country. The next generation will be better for knowing the path that allowed them to be in this world and enables them to shape the future.

All that being said, here are some ways you can get to studying your family line.

- **Ancestry is not the only game in town**. So, we've all heard about Ancestry at this point in terms of genealogy. I can tell you firsthand that it's a wonderful resource. If you have the money for it, short of hiring an actual genealogist, Ancestry is the way to go in terms of finding out where you come from. The site offers a bunch of different ways to access records in the name of building up your family tree. But as great as Ancestry is, it's by far not the only game in town. You can find several other paid sites, but there are a few free sites, such as MyHeritage and the Brister English Project, that specialize in researching African American families.

- **Don't discount the analog way of doing things.** Due to the unique nature of our history, you will find a lot of information using genealogy sites, mainly because someone else has done the footwork for you. But some details may be missed by those sites, such as death and birth certificates for people who have recently passed or been born, along with records of births written in Bibles and other odd places. Once upon a time, it wasn't uncommon to find information about a Christening in an old journal or photo album. In those cases, it's a good idea to contact the family matriarchs or patriarchs for connections that you might be missing. And when that option is available, libraries and library archives are incredible resources for familial information. You can find things such as yearbooks, newspaper articles, and census information in most library institutions. You'd be surprised at the wealth of information about your family that can be found in public spaces.

- **Keep track of your own history**. I think this one is harder to do now that we're in an almost entirely digital age. So many photos and records have been digitized on the web or the cloud or some other unseen and intangible source that I'm sure a lot of us are worried about their longevity. On that, I think the jury's out, as not enough time has passed for us to properly judge the effects of degradation, but that doesn't mean you shouldn't use as many sources as you can to preserve the good times. Outside of social media apps such as Facebook and Instagram, there are plenty of journal apps that you can use to preserve your memories. Or, if that's not your thing, there's no shame in keeping scrapbooks to preserve memories. It seems a little old school, but some of us enjoy having memories we can touch with our hands, and there's nothing wrong with that.

- **Don't hide the past**. This is something I learned

from a very good friend of mine. If you think about it, learning about your family means that you might unearth something you don't like or didn't want to know, but let me urge you against burying whatever it is even further. As human beings, we're messy. We cheat on our spouses, have babies out of wedlock, commit crimes, and embarrass our entire families. And it's all a part of your family's story. All of it. Who you are right now is comprised of all the good and the bad in your family. It all led up to you being right here and right now. Don't deny it. It's already a part of you. Plus, it makes for great storytelling at family functions.

The Time to Rise Up

How many times have you looked at what's happening around you socially and politically and felt some type of way about it? As black women, we're quick to kiki with our friends about the state of our country and how it affects us, but how many of us are out there with boots on the ground?

Now, I'm not judging you if you've never been out at the protests or given money to campaigns or ever done anything to actively promote change. There are a lot of reasons why we, as black women, might not be so eager to step up to the plate when it comes to making change. I probably don't have to tell you that one of the major reasons is that we don't feel like we're being heard within the social and political arenas. And if you feel like that, I cannot and will not blame you.

The fact of the matter is that black women are statistically ignored when it comes to social movements (American Psychological Association 2020), which is a shame because what the world needs to know about us and our opinions about the changes in the world is that we tend to be right on a lot of issues, and some of our white counterparts are noticing. When discussing how 53 percent of white women casted votes for former President Donald Trump in 2016 while a whopping 94 percent of black women voted for Hilary Clinton (CNN. com 2016), Comedian Chelsea Handler once urged white people to "vote like black women" (Scaccia 2018), because the one thing we're not about to do is vote against our best interests. That is to say, when it comes to issues that matter, black women don't tend to vote in a way that harms our community on the whole. And issues within the African American community often intersect with national issues (such as various issues surrounding human rights and inequality).

To put it in layman's terms, black women, by and large, do not vote for our elected officials like we're voting for Prom Queen. We don't choose the prettiest, most charismatic candidates. Half the time, we don't even *like* the person we're voting for (I can't tell you how many times I heard "We liked her husband! Not *her*!" back in 2016). The reason we don't vote that way is that we've been taught from the time we were small about the value of voting for the right people. Our relatives literally fought the police in the streets just to have that right.

Whether that's because we're actively involved or just because we see what's happening right outside our window, we've got the pulse of what needs changing in America. So, keep all that in mind when you're planning your political involvement. You're an important voice within the masses.

- **Speak on it!** The one thing that I think those of us over fifty are reluctant to get into and commit fully to is having a social media account. I think that a lot of us still think apps like TikTok and Twitter are a young person's game and we should stay away. I implore you, though, to reconsider.

Having an active social media platform these days is how most politicians get attention and get elected mostly because it's where most young people get their news from around the world these days. It's also the place where you'll find plenty of activists looking to spread their message. Why? Because it works. If you want to get active in the world of social justice, you've got to go where they are. One caution for this tip: *Never post anything you wouldn't post on the front page of a newspaper and always do your research before posting a topic.* I can't tell you how many people have been "ratioed" out of the game for posting a half-baked opinion, so keep your receipts and always speak the truth.

- **Getting in formation**. Despite the fact that 93 percent of BLM protests were peaceful (ACLED 2020), there are plenty of people who swear that when black people protest, we automatically burn down our cities. That idea has become so pervasive that some of us actually believe it. Obviously, you should do whatever you can to stay safe, but don't let what you've heard stop you from getting out there and protesting. Also, consider organizing a protest instead of just showing up for one. Start talking to others in your community and use that new social media account to gather supporters. You'll be surprised who shows up for you when you start to stand up against injustice.

- **Heels on the groundwork just as well as boots.** Okay, so let's say you're not into marching and protesting. For any number of reasons, that might not be it for a lot of us. There are a million different ways to show your support and make change in your community. You can donate to causes and organizations that help your community, or reach out to your local library and talk to the administrative staff and library board about creating programs for the black community that might be lacking in your neighborhood. You can make small efforts like volunteering with your local chapter of the NAACP or any civil rights organization. Start a drive at your local church to help black homeless youth. The list goes on and on. We can make real change within our communities in so many different ways, so look for options that work for you.

Remember Your Crown

I think it's easy for us to forget where we are in our family. We've spent so much time in other roles. We have been children, nieces, cousins, mothers, and wives, and now we are grandmothers and great-grandmothers even. We've seen so much of the world, and we've watched so many things go by that I think it's easy to get stuck in the time periods where we felt the most relevant.

But we *are* relevant right now! Black women over fifty are vibrant, beautiful, and healthy, *and* we now have enough wisdom to share with the rest of our world. We are a unique breed that's brand new to the modern world. If you doubt me, just consider the fact that Viola Davis was just in *The Woman King* doing backflips and fighting with staff, and she's fifty-eight years old.

You are the blueprint, black woman. We are strong and smart, and we have the benefit of remembering our ancestors to boot. No one is more worthy than we are to pass on the great legacy of our people. So take my advice when I tell you that it's time to learn it, live it, and love it.

Smooth Criminal

There's a coffee shop around the corner from Mirna's house that sells books and vintage reading materials. It's just a little mom and pop on an obscure street that she stops by every so often to get some tea and read whatever book she happens to be into.

One Sunday afternoon, Mirna finished the current novel she was reading and decided she wanted to get a new book from the coffee shop. While she was looking through the fiction section, she happened to see a display in the newspaper archive section surrounding criminals from the twenties and thirties. She thought it was interesting, so she had a look. In that section was a newspaper article about the famed "Bumpy Johnson," a crime boss from the 1930s and 40s. As she looked through the article, she was shocked to see a photo of a woman she'd seen all her life.

The woman was her grandmother as a child, sitting with Bumpy Johnson himself. They were at a block party event and her grandmother was taking an ice cream cone from Bumpy. Mirna was flabbergasted. She knew her family was from New York, but she had no idea that anyone in her family knew any crime bosses.

Mirna bought the newspaper article and read through it. Apparently, it was from a block party that, at the time, was being funded by local "entrepreneur" Bumpy Johnson. According to the caption, the photo was of Bumpy and his niece. *Niece??* She couldn't believe what she was reading and had to know what the real story was behind it. She feared for a moment that she would never find out as her grandmother had long passed away.

So, she called her mother and asked if she knew anything about her mother's childhood in Harlem. Her mother stated that she didn't, but she did know that her great-grandparents had several sons who were in and out of jail. Mirna told her mother what she found out, which prompted them to embark on a quest to uncover the real story behind Bumpy Johnson and her grandmother.

Not knowing where to start, they went to her uncle's house, as he had many of her grandmother's old belongings. They went through boxes and boxes of old albums and keepsakes before they found a box of newspaper clippings. Most of them were from various things and events, but quite a few were of the infamous gangster.

They dug some more, even inviting a genealogist to help them, and what they found out was that Bumpy

Johnson was, indeed, Mirna's great-great uncle. Her grandmother's family discovered what he did for a living shortly before they left New York and decided to disassociate themselves from him. But to Mirna, it looked as though her grandmother had not been able to let go of the memories of her uncle, who it seemed she knew as being a kind and generous man.

Upon finding this out, certain members of her family insisted that she never tell anyone about their wayward uncle and that it should be kept a secret. But Mirna was now interested in learning about who Bumpy was outside of his criminal life. What she learned was that while he was a criminal, he was also an activist, particularly after his final arrest in the sixties. Suddenly, Mirna saw the connection in her own life with her job as a campaign manager and social activist.

So, Mirna decided that this was a part of her family's legacy and should be told and shared. To this day, she keeps her grandmother's old belongings as a way to remember every piece of the puzzle of who they really are.

CHAPTER TEN

The Stride

"I designed a pyramid so tough that a star that only glows every one hundred years falls into the center giving divine perfect light. I am bad."

— Nikki Giovanni, "Ego Tripping"

The New Twenty

I know it's kind of cliché to call fifty the new twenty, but in a lot of ways, it actually is. The rules that we all grew up with have changed. The age of black women being seen as angry or disrespectful is ending. We are moving into a new era where we are celebrated for everything that we are, and you can see it in our fashion, media, and almost everywhere. Black women are at the forefront of a new wave of what strength, femininity, resilience, and wisdom represent to the human race. We are spiritual earth mothers and warrior goddesses. We are business owners and community leaders, and we cannot be silenced or stopped.

Yeah, okay, I am gassing you up, but am I wrong? When you look in the mirror at your enviously smooth skin, don't you see who you are and who you represent? The stories of our ancestors can be seen through our eyes and heard in our voices. Right now is the best time of our lives because we have become everything that we wanted to be when we were younger. I said it earlier, and I'll say it again. We are the blueprint and it's time for us to live up to that.

Not Your Mother's Mother's Life

When I was young, my grandmother did her best to teach me all the lessons she learned about being a proper young lady. When I went to church with her, I had to wear a slip under my dress and tights up until I was a teenager (at which time I was allowed to wear stockings). No nail polish or makeup was allowed, and all adults were to be addressed as Mrs. or Mr. (even up until I became an adult).

Looking back, it all seemed pretty restrictive. As if all those things could determine whether or not I was a lady. When I got older, I started to wonder what might happen if I didn't wear a slip with my skirt. Or if I decided to go barelegged in the summertime. Would my ancestors strike me down for my brazenness?

Well, I don't wear slips anymore, and these days, I tend to go barelegged more often than not and I'm still here. Society hasn't stoned me to death yet. So what does that mean? Has it ever mattered? Well, it must have at some point in time for my grandmother to feel it was so important. So what's changed?

I'll tell you what's changed. The world. *This* world. Black women and what they value have changed. Many of us are changing with it. What's fascinating is that, unlike most times in modern history, we're moving with the changes. Representation for us looks different. Older black actresses are being viewed as the standard more and more every day. I could go on and on about the front-runners in my mind, but here are just a few who you can look to:

- **Queen Angela**. If black people have any kind of royalty, Angela Bassett is our reigning queen. Her career spans at least three decades, and when she was at an age where Hollywood was telling women that they were not sexy enough anymore. When they were casting Meryl Streep in roles for older women, Angela Bassett was doing stunt choreography in movies like *Strange Days* and tearing it up on stage in *What's Love Got to Do With It?* She's a shining example of what a black woman in her sixties can achieve. (You heard me right. *Sixties!*) She is a master of her craft and the main draw every time she walks on screen.

- **The Jane of All Trades**. Do you know who Stacey Abrams is? If not, you should. Stacey Abrams rose to fame when she ran for the gubernatorial election in Georgia in 2018. She became the first black woman to do it and only narrowly lost the election. However, that defeat did little to stop her momentum. Her accomplishments include voting rights activist, lawyer, advocate for human rights in, well, every way that counts, *and* she's a best-selling author. Abrams is the standard for building your legacy and giving your life over to the greater good of your community. If she ever runs for President, she's already got my vote.

- **Horror Noire Queen**. Horror writers typically come in one flavor and one flavor only: white and male. That's the way of the world for most genres in the way of novels but especially horror and sci-fi and fantasy. However, there's one writer who is breaking those barriers. Tananarive Due, author of *The Living Blood* and *The Good House,* is not only in a league of her own when it comes to the genre, but she's also a film historian who teaches a course on racism within the horror genre at UCLA. If you like a good scare and are not familiar with her work, I strongly suggest you check her out.

- **The Warrior Goddess.** No offense to anybody reading this, but if you don't know who Angela Davis is, where have you been all these years? Angela Davis has been fighting for black independence and has been a prominent woman in the civil rights movement since she was a young woman in the 60s. She's run for Vice President twice, and if there's a movement out there for our people, you better believe she's right there up front and center. When I think of black women of our generation who have committed their lives to the betterment of society and our people, Ms. Davis is front and center in everywhere you could imagine.

And I could go on. Honestly, those are just my top four when I think about women who have and continue to pave the way for the rest of America. I could fill this book with names, actually, but those are just a few whose lives you can study and relate to when you're trying to find your role in this world.

It's All Uphill from Here

As I mentioned at the beginning of this book, my outlook on this chapter of my life did not start out all sunshine and roses. Like many of you, I wanted to resist getting old for as long as possible. It was as if there was a time limit on my life all of a sudden. For a while, I was focusing on my sudden lack of summers instead of the only summer that really mattered, which was the one I was living in right then. I could only picture myself as being decrepit, old, and a burden on my family.

I'm not going to lie, I was in a bad place for a long time. I didn't want to be old, mostly because I just didn't feel old. I could still dance at parties. I looked in the mirror and saw a beautiful, desirable woman. I didn't see this ancient Methuselah that everyone seemed to think we all turn into at a certain point. I was still young and vibrant, dammit!

And then something happened that changed my entire perspective. My husband and I had been planning a trip out of the country for months. He had wanted to travel to Africa for as long as I've known him, and we finally had enough money and time to go. Even though I didn't feel much like sitting on a plane for sixteen plus hours, it was my husband's dream, and I was determined to see him experience it.

When we landed in Kenya, something happened from the moment I set foot inside the airport. I can't explain it in any other way than I felt like I had just come home. You know how when you've gotten off a long flight and you get back to your home city and everything feels familiar to you? Maybe it was the smell of the air, the feeling of the warmth on my skin when we walked outside. I don't know. But for a second, I thought that somehow the flight had turned around and set us back down in America.

From that point on, we explored everything that Kenya had to offer. We went on safari in the Maasai

Mara and met with members of the Maasai. We observed how everyone lived a calm and peaceful life that was so different from what we were used to. At night, we went into the city and enjoyed the music in the clubs. Afrobeats thumped rhythmically, like the beating of a heart.

I've heard that many people have had a similar experience when going to the cradle of our civilization. In fact, I distinctly remember Paul Simon talking about it way back in the 80s when he went to South Africa. He was so inspired by the sights and sounds that he created the album "Graceland" in honor of it. When it came out, I didn't think much of it. To a child's ears, it sounded a little hokey. It wasn't until I was in Africa that I felt what he undoubtedly must have felt.

I felt life. A heartbeat under the ground that matched my own and the breath of my ancestors in the wind. And being there, I started to see my worth as a black woman and as a human being. My life is not the sum of my youth. My life is everything that I was, everything I am, and everything I will ever become.

I came back with a new perspective. I wasn't getting "old." I was hitting my stride. I'm still the vibrant woman I've always been, but I'm wiser now. I'm more connected to this place I'm in. And most importantly, I value the breath I take in so much more. Today, I stand ten toes down in my greatness and all of you do too. The best part is that hopefully, you won't have to travel all the way to Africa to find out.

You are a black woman in the diamond years of her life. Don't ever forget how incredible you truly are.

In Conclusion

"I'm the bar."

— Beyonce, "Alien Superstar"

A s I told you at the beginning of this book, my mother, Ms. Miriam, was a free spirit. I've been thinking a lot about her as I write this, and as I end this book, I am reminded of one of the last times we spoke.

It was Thanksgiving and we all were having dinner at her house. That year was a good one too. Everyone managed to make it in to visit. I saw aunts and uncles I haven't seen since I was a little girl. It was a glorious fellowship of my family's elders with the newer generations, and I was so happy to be a part of it.

As will happen during gatherings within the black family, conversations will fly across the dinner table and beyond freely. No subject is taboo amongst adults. Religion and politics are a regular staple within our family, as I'm sure it is within just about every black family. On this particular holiday, three of the men in my family got into a fiery debate about women's health and the problem of implicit bias within the medical community. My aunt brought her boyfriend, a doctor and professor at the local university, who weighed in and mostly led the conversation (as it was his area of expertise).

They were all sitting in the living room, discussing it amongst themselves, when my mother walked in, bringing my father a cup of coffee and she joined the conversation. When I tell you that there was a hush that went over everyone in the room as she leveled out her opinions as she saw them...Boy, oh, boy. My mother made strong, intelligent points. She sparred with them not just as an equal, but as an intellectual just like all of them. I remember listening to them all talk and thinking to myself, *Why can't it always be that way outside of this room?*

The world doesn't like to listen to black women, and I believe it gets worse as we get older. There is an idea of who we're supposed to be within the American community, and if we don't fit in with that, then we're ignored. We lead the way on just about every social and political stage and still, we're ignored.

I think a lot about the contributions we, as black women, can make in this world. I believe, just as women, there is this narrative that when we reach a certain age, then that means it's time to hang it up and sit this one out. There's something about the intersectionality of being black, a woman, *and* over fifty that makes everyone think of us as losing our ability to contribute to this society.

And it's crazy to me because that could not be further from the truth. As women of color, we are the standard, and as such, we are living, breathing representations of a future to come. I know sometimes, it's hard to get your head around that. We came up in a world that has done ITS absolute best to make sure we never realized our true power and influence. Black women are the lifeblood of our people and of this country. Progress, influence, social justice, entertainment, and fashion—we are the bar. We always have been, and we always will be.

Ms. Miriam understood that dynamic outside of that living room on that Thanksgiving. She understood it because she was in touch with who she was and who people *thought* she was. She lived her life to subvert the opinions of everyone who thought that because she was too feminine or too black or too old, her thoughts and words didn't matter. She was intellectually healthy, spiritually fulfilled, and well-versed in the power of the gifts passed down to her from the ancestors who fought for her to speak her truth.

I believe that once we, as black women, understand that our gifts lie in our brilliance, then the rest will come. The future isn't so much ours to claim because it never left our possession. We are then, right now, and everything to come.

When she passed away, the one thing I remember the most was all the wonderful stories told about her at her homegoing. A lot were personal stories, but almost all pointed out her tenacity, her sense of freedom, and the fearless way she lived her life. Those stories left me with a picture of her as the quintessential black woman. As someone that I should aspire to be.

And that's what I think we should all want to leave for the next generation. Our unique position to be loud and proud enough to change the world we live in. To paraphrase Queen Bey, we are "One of One." Everyone aspires to be us because we are the bar.

Okay, so now that I've gassed you up, what are you waiting for? This is our world, and once we settle into our stride, everyone will fall in line. Let the tips and stories in this book lead you as our ancestors have always intended.

Be strong. Be Blessed. And always remember you are the bar.

References

AARP. 2018. "Romance Scams." AARP. Last modified December 3, 2018. https://www.aarp.org/money/scams-fraud/info-2019/romance.html?cmp=KNC-DSO-FRAUD-Ongoing-RomanceScams-8856-GOOG-ONGOING-DatingScams-Exact-NonBrand&gclid=CjwKCAjwzo2mBhAUEiwAf7wjkksnKG-QtDiKri7nhDQflqGPGDqIQUKHU8_pZi3EYBltlHxvnyk4pxoCbcoQAvD_BwE&gclsrc=aw.d.

ABC News. 2019. "Inside New Orleans' All-Female Motorcycle Club 'The Caramel Curves.'" YouTube video, New Orleans, March 12, 2019. https://www.youtube.com/watch?v=-V7a4qNKdkQ

ACLED. 2020. "Demonstrations and Political Violence in America: New Data for Summer 2020." ACLED. Last modified September 3, 2020. https://acleddata.com/2020/09/03/demonstrations-political-violence-in-america-new-data-for-summer-2020/.

American Psychological Association. 2020. "Black Women Often Ignored by Social Justice Movements." American Psychological Association. Last modified July 13, 2020. https://www.apa.org/news/press/releases/2020/07/black-women-social-justice.

Ancestry.com. 1997-2023. *Ancestry.* Accessed 2023. www.ancestry.com.

Arias, Elizabeth. 2022. "United States Life Tables, 2000: National Vital Statistics Reports." *National Center for Health Statistic.*

Bharmal, Nazleen, Chi-Hong Tseng, Robert Kaplan, and Mitchell D. Wong. 2012. "State-Level Variations in Racial Disparities in Live Expectancy." *Health Services Research* 544-555.

Brown-Riggs, Constance. 2022. "Maintaining Fitness After 50." BlackDoctor.org, January 29, 2022. https://blackdoctor.org/maintaining-fitness-after-50/.

Butrica, Barbara A., and Karen E. Smith. 2012. "Racial and Ethnic Differences in the Retirement Prospects of Divorced Women in the Baby Boom and Generation X Cohorts." *SSA.gov.* https://www.ssa.gov/policy/docs/ssb/v72n1/v72n1p23.html.

Butrica, Barbara A., and Karen E. Smith. 2012. "The Retirement Prospects of Divorced Women." *Social Security Bulletin* (72) 11-22.

Centers for Disease Control and Prevention. 2016. "Leading Causes of Death - Females - Non-Hispanic Black - United States, 2016." Centers for Disease Control and Prevention.. https://www.cdc.gov/women/lcod/2016/nonhispanic-black/index.htm.

Clemenson, G. 2020. "Enriching Hippocampal Memory Function in Older Adults through Video Games." *Behavioral Brain Research.* 390.

CNN.com. 2016. "Exit Polls." *CNN.* November 23. Accessed 2023. https://www.cnn.com/election/2016/results/exit-polls/national/president.

Cole, Deon. 2019. *Deon Cole: Cole Hearted.* Performed by Deon Cole. Belk Theatre, North Carolina.

Coles, Stewart M., Josh Pasek. 2020. "Intersectional Invisibility Revisited: How Group Prototypes Lead to the Erasure and Exclusion of Black Women." *Translational Issues in Psychological Science.* http://dx.doi.org/10.1037/tps0000256

Cowles, Anne, William W. Beatty, Sara J. Nixon, Lanna J. Lutz, Kayla Paulk, and Elliott D. Ross. 2003. "Musical Skill in Dementia: A Violinist Presumed to Have Alzheimer's Disease Learns to Play a New Song." *Neurocase* 493-503.

Dreisbach, Shaun. 2017. "50 States of Women." *Glamour,* August 1, 2017. https://www.glamour.com/story/50-states-of-women.

Findley, Caleigh A., Makayla F. Cox, Adam B. Lipson, Ratasha Bradley, Kevin N. Hascup, and Carla Yuede. 2023. "Health Disparities in Aging: Improving Dementia Care for Black Women." *Frontiers in Aging Neuroscience.*

Handwerk, Brian. 2022. "East Africa's Oldest Modern Fossil is Way Older Than Previously Thought." *Smithsonian Magazine,* January 12, 2022. https://www.smithsonianmag.com/science-nature/east-africas-oldest-modern-human-fossil-is-way-older-than-previously-thought-180979384/.

Healthy Back Bag. n.d. *Healthy Back Bag.* https://www.thehealthybackbag.co.uk/blog/11-excellent-alternative-exercise-ideas.

Hoffman, Kelly M., Sophie Trawalter, Jordan R. Axt, and M. Norman Oliver. 2016. "Racial Bias in Pain Assessment and Treatment Recommendations, and False Beliefs about Biological Differences Between Blacks and Whites." *National Library of Medicine.*

Hull, Megan. 2020. "Exposure Therapy at The Recovery Village Palm Beach." The Recovery Village at Baptist Health. Last modified July 15, 2020. https://www.floridarehab.com/treatment/addiction-therapies/exposure-therapy/.

Lee, Seonhwa, Kandauda K.A.S. Wickrama, Tae Kyoung Lee, and Catherine Walker O'Neal. 2021. "Long-Term Physical Health Consequences of Financial and Marital Stress in Middle-Aged Couples." *Journal of Marriage and Family* 1212-1226.

Lewis, Jenifer. 2018. *The Mother of Black Hollywood.* New York: Amistad.

Lockett, Eleesha. 2022. "Best Brain Stimulating Games for Dementia and Why They Work." *Healthline,* August 30, 2022. https://www.healthline.com/health/alzheimers-dementia/memory-games-for-dementia.

Lockett, Eleesha. 2023. "Why It's Time to Shift the Focus to Mental Health in the Black Community." *Healthline*, February 17, 2023. https://www.healthline.com/health/mental-health/mental-health-in-the-black-community.

Martínez, Nasha Addarich. 2023. "5 Reasons You Should Unplug from Social Media." *CNET,* March 7, 2023. https://www.cnet.com/health/mental/unplug-from-social-media/.

Mayer, Beth Ann. 2022. "Transcendental Meditation: The Beatles Did it, But Can It Help You?" *Healthline*, February 22, 2022. https://www.healthline.com/health/mind-body/transcendental-meditation.

Mayo Clinic. 2022. "Healthy Lifestyle: Nutrition and Healthy Eating." Mayo Clinic. Last modified October 12, 2022. https://www.mayoclinic.org/healthy-lifestyle/nutrition-and-healthy-eating/in-depth/water/art-20044256#:~:text=The%20U.S.%20National%20Academies%20of,fluids%20a%20day%20for%20women.

Mendez, Mario F. 2019. "Bilingualism and Dementia: Cognitive Reserve to Linguistic Competency." *Journal of Alzheimer's Disease* 377-388.

Merriam-Webster.com Dictionary, s.v.. "bucket list," https://www.merriam-webster.com/dictionary/bucket%20list.

MyHeritage.com. 2023. *MyHeritage*. Accessed 2023. www.myheritage.com.

National Institute on Aging. 2021. "What Is Menopause?" National Institute on Aging. Last Modified September 30, 2021. https://www.nia.nih.gov/health/what-menopause#:~:text=The%20menopausal%20transition%20most%20often,begins%2C%20and%20race%20and%20ethnicity.

Pillai, Jagan A., Charles B. Hall, Dennis W. Dickson, Herman Buschke, Richard B. Lipton, and Joe Verghese. 2014. "Association of Crossword Puzzle Participation with Memory Decline in Persons Who Develop Dementia." *National Library of Medicine.*

Prince Harry, The Duke of Sussex. 2023. *Spare.* New York: Penguin Random House.

Reiner, Rob, director. *The Bucket List.* Warner Bros., 2007, 1 hr., 37 min.

Rodgers, Rachel. 2021. *We Should All Be Millionaires.* Nashville: Harper Collins Leadership.

Rose, Adam. 2023. *9 Money Habits Keeping You Poor.* A&T Publishing.

Royal, James. 2023. "11 Best Investment Apps in August 2023." *Bankrate,* August 15, 2023. https://www.bankrate.com/investing/best-investment-apps/.

Scaccia, AnnaMarya. 2018. "Chelsea Handler Calls on White Women to Vote with Black Women." *Romper,* October 22, 2018. https://www.romper.com/p/chelsea-handler-calls-on-white-women-to-vote-with-black-women-in-the-midterm-elections-12644502.

Schweizer, Valerie. 2019. "Marriage to Divorce Ratio in the U.S.: Demographic Variation, 2018." *Family Profiles* 19-27. https://www.bgsu.edu/ncfmr/resources/data/family-profiles/schweizer-marriage-divorce-ratio-demo-variation-fp-19-27.html.

The Brister English Project. 2023. *The Brister English Project.* Accessed 2023. www.bristerep.me.

Tongco, Tricia. 2016. "Searching Google for 'Beautiful Woman' Reveals Biases." *ATTN:,* August 12, 2016. https://archive.attn.com/stories/10611/google-searching-beautiful-woman-reveals-racism.

U.S. Government Accountability Office. "Women in the Workforce: The Gender Pay Gap is Greater for Certain Racial and Ethnic Groups and Varies by Educational Level." Washington: GAO, 2022. https://www.gao.gov/products/gap-23-106041.

Vogels, Emily A., and Colleen McClain. 2023. "Key Findings About Online Dating in the U.S." *Pew Research Center*, February 2, 2023. https://www.pewresearch.org/short-reads/2023/02/02/key-findings-about-online-dating-in-the-u-s/.

Wiley, Cherese. 2016. "Surprising Health Benefits of Marriage." *Baylor Scott and White Health*, November 7, 2016. https://www.bswhealth.com/blog/surprising-health-benefits-marriage#:~:text=A%20study%20earlier%20this%20year,single%20and%20develop%20the%20disease.

Woods, Paris. 2021. *The Black Girl's Guide to Financial Freedom: Build Wealth, Retire Early, and Live the Life of Your Dreams.* Houston: Freedom Unlimited, LLC.

About the Author

Nia J. Rivers is a retired professor of African American Studies and literature. She is also a life coach and focuses on inspirational and spiritual teachings to women who aspire to live happy and healthy lives. Nia has traveled the world through speaking engagements on racial diversity, media literacy, and empowerment for black women everywhere. She continues to enlighten and educate wherever she goes.

Currently, she hosts a weekly workshop for black women over fifty in her home state of Michigan. Nia is a prolific writer and poet and has dedicated her life to the betterment of black women. She is a firm believer that black women and women of color are the lifeblood of the nation and has a vested interest in preserving the rich culture that comes with African American women.

Nia is happily married to her husband, poet and filmmaker David Rivers. She is also the mother of three beautiful children, as well as a grandmother to five grandchildren. In her spare time, Nia enjoys writing fiction, practicing Yoga and meditation, and performing poetry with her husband David at her local coffee shop. They also have three dogs and resides in Kalamazoo, Michigan.

Author Note

Thank you for purchasing and reading my book. I am extremely grateful and hope you found value in reading it. Please consider sharing it with friends or family and leaving a review online. Your feedback and support are always ap-preciated and allow me to continue doing what I love. Please go to Amazon if you'd like to leave a review.